A PORTRAIT OF
BLACKPOOL
AND THE FYLDE

JON SPARKS

HALSGROVE

First published in Great Britain in 2007

British Library Cataloguing-in-Publication Data
A CIP record for this title is available from the British Library

ISBN 978 1 84114 601 0

HALSGROVE
Halsgrove House
Ryelands Farm Industrial Estate
Bagley Green, Wellington
Somerset TA21 9PZ
T: 01823 653777
F: 01823 216796
email: sales@halsgrove.com
website: www.halsgrove.com

Printed and bound by D'Auria Industrie Grafiche Spa, Italy

INTRODUCTION

Everyone knows Blackpool, or at least has an image of the place: kiss-me-quick hats, aproned landladies, Illuminations, George Formby's little stick of Blackpool Rock. If you look for cliches you can certainly find them and in fact I suppose Blackpool has been cheerfully living up to expectations for at least a century and a half.

Its fame and fortune were based on two things: railways, and the week's holiday granted to the Lancashire mill workers. It's hardly possible to overstate what Blackpool must have meant to those workers; not just a fleeting escape from drudgery, but freedom, space and fresh air (given Blackpool's breezy climate, maybe a little too fresh at times!).

Most of Lancashire's mills have disappeared or been converted to other uses. Blackpool still has its rail connections, though most of today's visitors come by car. However, it's cheap air travel and the foreign package holiday that have posed the biggest challenge to Blackpool's traditional sources of income. There's a certain irony in the fact that substantial numbers of people now start their foreign holidays from Blackpool's own airport (while rather fewer visitors from Spain or Portugal return the favour).

Blackpool has worked hard to reinvent itself and has successfully maintained its position as Britain's leading seaside resort. It's Blackpool Pleasure Beach, not Buckingham Palace, that is Britain's most visited tourist attraction – a fact I find oddly pleasing. Whether or not its rides appeal, the Pleasure Beach now rivals Blackpool Tower itself as a dominant feature of the landscape.

If much has changed, there's also much that hasn't, like the enduring and endearing tram system. And then there are the sea breezes, the miles of sand, and the glorious sunsets. Everyone may think they know Blackpool, but there is much more to discover.

Blackpool itself is really only the centre-piece of a conurbation which lines the entire west-facing coastline of this part of Lancashire, stretching more than 20km from Lytham to Fleetwood. Technically, Blackpool itself is no longer in Lancashire but a self-contained authority, but these niceties have little impact on the real landscape.

If everyone thinks they know Blackpool, the same cannot be said of its rural hinterland. Mention the Fylde and few from outside Lancashire will have a clue where you mean. Most visitors head straight for the coast, crossing the Fylde almost without noticing, and if they do glance out of the window of their Pendolino may take it as an unremarkable and largely flat piece of country.

Again, there is far more to it than meets the eye. The Fylde is subtle in its attractions, and may take a little time to get to know, but gradually reveals a surprising variety of landscape and habitat. There are places within a few kilometres of Blackpool Tower where dragonflies abound and ospreys have been sighted. There is rich farmland that a couple of centuries ago was still swamp; drainage channels and the stumps of numerous windmills testify to the profound changes that have been wrought on the landscape. In a few places one can still glimpse what that primeval wetland might have been like, most notably along Crawley's Dyke, near Pilling.

Because the land is generally flat, the horizon is relatively close, yet paradoxically the Fylde feels unusually spacious. Perhaps it's the big skies, or perhaps it's just that you need not feel overlooked. It's not a wilderness, and you are never very far from a road or a house, but still one can have that sense of getting away from it all.

Blackpool and the Fylde may seem like chalk and cheese, but perhaps they have more in common than is immediately apparent. The agricultural richness of the Fylde, and the harvest of the seas at Fleetwood, underpinned Blackpool's early development, and economically they are still interdependent. But if there is one overarching quality that they share, it is surely that sense of space.

Jon Sparks

Breaking wave, Blackpool
One of the highest tides of the year combined with an onshore
wind and midday sun to produce exhilarating conditions.

Beach detail, Fleetwood
Worn, weathered and stubborn, these old timbers were full of texture.

Beach detail, Rossall
The crumpled iron stanchion is mute
evidence of the power of the sea.

The White Church, St Anne's
The White Church is one of the Fylde's most unusual buildings: Edwardian in date and sometimes described as Byzantine in style, its dome and minaret make it look more like a mosque. It is in fact a United Reformed church.

Opposite: **Under Central Pier, Blackpool**
Opened in 1868, Central Pier was the second of Blackpool's three piers and became known as the 'people's pier' while the North Pier (seen in the distance) attracted a more genteel clientele.

View from Head Nook Bridge
The flatness of most of the Fylde makes it difficult to get wide views and
high points are at a premium. Head Nook Bridge, on the Lancaster Canal near
Bilsborrow, gave a handy extra few metres of elevation.

The Windmill, Lytham
There are still many windmills in the Fylde; most of them were originally used
to drive drainage pumps. The mill at Lytham is the best known and is distinguished
by the definite article. It now houses a small museum.

Tram station, Little Bispham
This was one of several shelters or stations built in the 1920s
during a period of expansion of the tram network.

Opposite: **Sunset, Wyre Estuary**
A winter sunset from near Shard Bridge, looking towards Little Thornton.

St Chad's church, Poulton-le-Fylde
St Chad's church can trace its history
back to Norman times but the bulk of the
fabric seen today is eighteenth century.

'Welcome Home'
Intended to commemorate the 'heroic lives of Fleetwood's fishermen
and their families', this sculpture, by Anita Lafford, stands at a spot
where families still watch for the return of loved ones.

Frost on maize, near Singleton
In little more than a decade maize has become a very
significant crop for the farmers of the Fylde.

Fruit bowl, Cleveleys
The kiosk below was closed when I took this picture so
I wasn't able to establish if they really sold fresh fruit.

Victoria Street, Blackpool
Victoria Street runs between the Promenade and
the Winter Gardens.

Opposite: **North Shore, Blackpool**
It was a hot day: at full magnification this image
clearly shows the rippling effect of the heat.

Breaking wave, Bispham
There are times when landscape photography turns into
action photography and this was one of them.

Marram grass, St Anne's
Marram grass is the quintessential plant of young dune systems
and plays a crucial role in binding the sand.

Sea aster, by Wrea Brook
Sea aster *(Aster tripolium)* is a common plant of salt-marsh,
here found between Lytham and Warton.

Opposite: **Lapwings and hot-air balloon**
A flight of lapwings (also known as peewits) and
a more distant hot-air balloon over the Fylde.

Sunset over the Irish Sea
I watched for the proverbial 'green flash' but had no luck, and on
reviewing my shots I preferred this one with the sun obscured.

Opposite: **Fleetwood from Knott End**
This view is taken across the mouth of the River Wyre. Queen's Terrace is a major feature of Fleetwood's
nineteenth-century planned townscape. On the left is one of the Stena ferries which ply twice
daily to Larne in Northern Ireland, and on the right is the Pharos Lighthouse.

25

Frosty morning, near Singleton
The low-angled light at the beginning and end of the day really
does help in picking out features in flat country.

The Winter Gardens, Blackpool
The Winter Gardens complex, opened in 1878, sprawls over a 6-acre site.
It houses a ballroom, theatre, opera house and arena, and regularly hosts
major political party conferences and other events.

Lion, Stanley Park, Blackpool
I thought this lion had an
unusually friendly look.

Willows, Warton Brows
This was a strange location, with desolate saltmarsh to one side while on the other was the
BAE aerodrome at Warton, from which jets on test occasionally screamed into the sky.

Reeds, River Wyre
I found these reeds on a stretch of the Wyre Way a few
kilometres inland from Shard Bridge.

Opposite: **Promenade and Pleasure Beach**
Blackpool's Illuminations have been staged every autumn, with wartime interruptions,
since 1912, and still attract many thousands of visitors (and photographers!).

Skippool Creek
Skippool Creek, off the River Wyre, is fascinating; there are over a hundred
wooden jetties, all different, and many as ramshackle as this one.

Opposite: **Metal detectorist, Blackpool**
I suppose there are rich pickings for the detectorist on a beach
like Blackpool's, with the waves bringing some finds and the
forgetfulness of holidaymakers yielding many more.

Blackpool Tower
Blackpool Tower was opened in 1894 and stands 158 metres tall. It's often said to have been intended as a rival to the Eiffel Tower, though it is only about half as tall and is by no means an exact replica.

Wrea Green
Wrea Green has the largest village green in Lancashire and indeed one of the largest in
the country. It has been photographed many times and I was keen to find a different angle.

Black Bull, Great Eccleston
This nice example of a traditional pub sign is in Great Eccleston, a lively village at the heart of the Fylde.

Dragonfly
This is a male Common Darter dragonfly *(Sympetrum striolatum)*,
resting obligingly on a fence near Warton.

Crawley's Dyke
Nowhere gives a better insight into how the Fylde must have once looked than
the area alongside Crawley's Dyke, between Winmarleigh and Pilling.

Opposite: **The Fylde from Preesall**
Preesall stands on the most abrupt hill in the Fylde, making it an unusually fine viewpoint.

Cartford Bridge
Cartford Bridge, over the River Wyre, is the last
surviving toll bridge in the Fylde.

Opposite: **Cyclist, Island Lane**
The flat terrain of the Fylde makes for easy cycling –
at least when the wind isn't blowing!

Misty evening near Nateby
Low-lying and moist, the Fylde is quite prone to the formation of mist, and
these are some of the best times to photograph its subtle landscapes.

Opposite: **View towards the Bowland Fells**
A long lens compresses the distance to the heights of the
Bowland Fells, with Hawthornthwaite Fell prominent here.

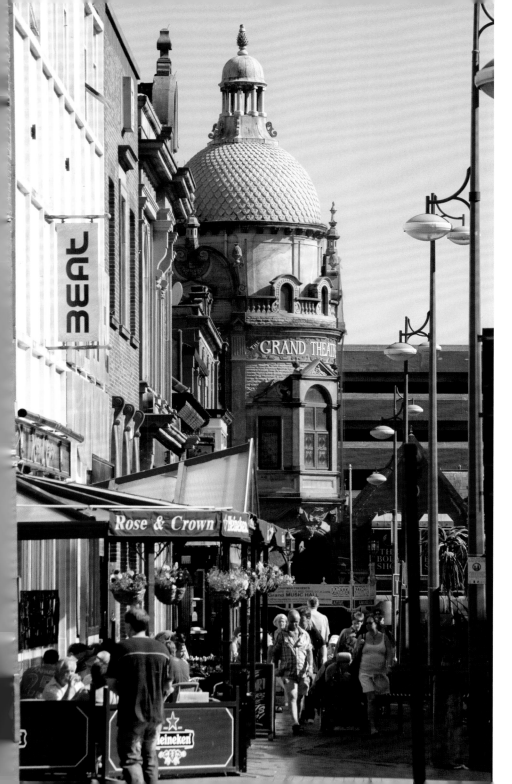

Corporation Street, Blackpool
A busy scene, with the dome of the
Grand Theatre on the skyline.

Open-top tram
Blackpool's tram network dates back to 1885, when it was a global pioneer
of electric traction. It is also the only tram network in Britain to have functioned
continuously right up to the present day. This open-top car is known as a 'boat' tram.

Trawler at Fleetwood
In its heyday Fleetwood was England's leading deep-sea fishing port but the industry today is much reduced;
as recently as 1982 over 12,000 tonnes of fish were landed; the figure for 2005 was a mere 570 tonnes.

Marton Mere
Marton Mere, on the outskirts of Blackpool, is a Local Nature Reserve, noted
for wildflowers including several species of orchid. It is also a good place for butterflies
and of course birds including bittern, marsh harrier and the occasional visiting osprey.

Blackpool Tower, detail
It is curious how showing just a
section of something can often give
a better impression of scale than the
whole. It also highlights the superb
intricacy of the Tower's
Victorian ironwork.

Opposite: **Waders, Pilling Sands**
The resting birds are mostly lapwing,
those on the wing are knot.

Skippool Creek
I make no excuses for including more than one shot of Skippool Creek, which
strikes me as one of the most unusual and surprising spots in the entire area.

Canal fringe
A wide variety of plants colonise the fringes of the Lancaster Canal
(this is near Salwick). Here are common reed and the club-like
reed-mace – commonly referred to as 'bulrush' although it is
nothing like the true bulrush.

Canada geese, St Anne's
Canada geese are a familiar sight, with a breeding population as well as winter visitors.
The vast expanse of St Anne's Sands can be seen in the background.

Opposite: **Donkey-ride, Blackpool**
Many of the classic British seaside traditions are alive and
well in Blackpool; the Central Pier is seen behind.

Sacred Heart church, Blackpool
The Sacred Heart of Jesus and Mary, to give it its full name, was founded in 1851 and stands on Talbot Square in the centre of Blackpool. My eye was drawn by the unusual detail of this lantern.

Turnstone, Cleveleys
Turnstone are among the more approachable of waders,
but I still kept my distance and used a long lens.

Post-box, Catterall Lane
With an EIIR insignia, this post-box
cannot be much over fifty years old, but
that has been more than long enough
for the tree to grow around it.

Marsh Mill, Thornton
The tower of Marsh Mill stands 23m high, making it one of the tallest in the Fylde. Many Fylde mills were built to pump water from the low-lying land but Marsh Mill was a flour mill. It was built in 1794 and recently restored; it now houses a milling museum and is the centrepiece of Marsh Mill Village, a collection of restaurants and speciality shops.

Puffball fungus, near Winmarleigh
At first I thought this was a discarded child's
football lying in the field, but closer inspection
showed it to be a huge puffball fungus.

Opposite: **View towards Beacon Fell**
A view from fields west of Bilsborrow
to Beacon Fell. This isolated 266m hill is a
popular country park and has expansive
views, not least over the Fylde.

Radio masts, Inskip
The Fylde is full of surprises, so it's typical to find a Royal Navy base more than 15km
from the sea: this is RNWS Inskip, used for communications with the fleet.

Opposite: **Shoreline at Cleveleys**
A breezy evening, looking south towards Blackpool. The massive white
Norbreck Castle Hotel is almost as prominent as the Tower.

Old tractor, Lytham
This is one of several old tractors used to reach boats in the shallow waters off Lytham.

Illuminations, Blackpool
From small beginnings in 1912, Blackpool's Illuminations today stretch almost ten kilometres, from Starr Gate to Bispham. The season runs from roughly the end of August to the beginning of November.

Wave, Rossall
Evening light lit up the waves breaking along the Rossall shore.

Opposite: **Reflections, beside the Wyre**
I walked a stretch of the Wyre Way upstream from Shard Bridge and
didn't see another soul until the next road, about 5km on.

Sunset, South Shore
Many of the best sunset shots are actually taken after the sun has set, when
the contrast is less extreme and the colours often develop more fully.

Morning, Catterall Hall
A useful footbridge crosses the River Wyre just above
Catterall Hall and close to the tiny village of Churchtown.

Drug Store, Blackpool
In fact, the Imperial Drug Store – by Royal Appointment?

Blackpool Tower and tram
This may be a cliched image of
Blackpool, but I couldn't resist.

Old log, near Shard Bridge
Evening light picked out the weathered texture of the wood as well as its colony of bracket fungus.

Opposite: **Nets, Pilling Lane**
These are not fishing nets, as you might think, but are there to protect soft fruit.

The Lancaster Canal
Having arbitrarily declared it as the
boundary of the Fylde, I thought
I should include an image of the
canal, in this case near Bilsborrow.

Full Moon and Big Dipper
Officially known as the Pepsi Max Big One, when it opened in 1994 it was the
tallest and fastest roller-coaster in the world, but has since been overtaken by foreign
competitors. At 65m it is still the highest in Britain and second highest in Europe.

Cottages in Kirkham
Kirkham and Poulton are the only inland towns in the Fylde.

Lower Lighthouse, Fleetwood
Standing on the sea-front the Lower Lighthouse was built in 1840. By lining it up with the Pharos Lighthouse (page 134) navigators can be sure they are in the deep channel.

Pylons, near Winmarleigh
Apart from the Inskip radio masts (page 60)
these are the tallest things in the Fylde.

Detail, Winter Gardens
Blackpool's Winter Gardens are on a monumental scale but, like so many
Victorian buildings, there's also a lot of fine detail to appreciate.

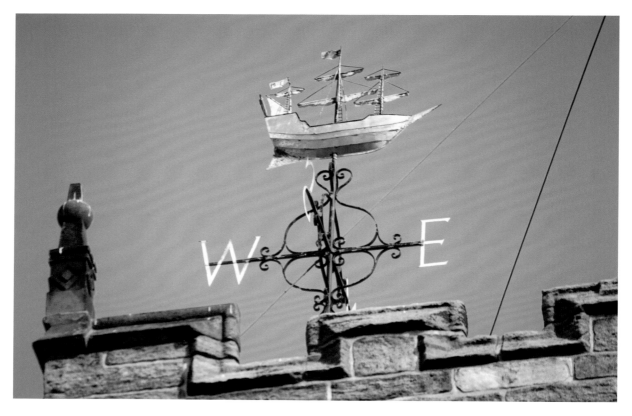

Weather vane, Poulton-le-Fylde
This attractive weather-vane crowns St Chad's church, Poulton-le-Fylde.

Opposite: **Waves, St Anne's**
A low winter sun caught the crests of the waves.

The Windmill, Lytham
The Windmill stands in splendid isolation
on the Green at Lytham, apart from the
old lifeboat station adjoining.

Opposite: **Fylde morning**
The fields of the Fylde sweep away
to a horizon of the Bowland Fells,
with Fair Snape Fell and Parlick to
the left of the picture.

Wave on steps, Blackpool
In more benign conditions these steps give
access to the beach, but not on this occasion!

Opposite: **Sea-angler, North Shore**
It was a rough day – definitely one for the
anglers to be well wrapped up. I'm not sure
how good it was for catching anything.

Reed-beds, Marton Mere
Common reed *(Phragmites australis)* dominates the fringes of
the mere. Blackpool Tower is about 4km distant.

Stubble patterns
The lines and colours of the stubble in this field
prompted me to make a near-abstract image.

St Michael's on Wyre
The church has a history dating back to the Saxon period. The village was originally
called Upper Rawcliffe but came to be referred to by the name of its church.

Hawthorn shadows
In a car, or even on a bike, you may appreciate the broader landscape
but little details like this are usually seen only by the traveller on foot.

Mirror-ball, South Shore
This is an intriguing feature on the Prom opposite the Solaris Centre;
I wasn't the only photographer playing with its visual possibilities.

Opposite: **Blackpool from Central Pier**
A classic view; the Tower, North Pier, hot sun and people enjoying themselves.

The Carneddau from Blackpool
The Lake District hills are often seen from Blackpool; the heights of the
Carneddau, in Snowdonia, are more distant and require a clearer day.

Grange Hill Wood
This was a chilly morning, but a fruitful one.

Grand Theatre, Blackpool.
Designed by Frank Matcham and completed in 1894, the 1200-seat theatre is now a Grade II listed building and is undergoing major restoration.

Opposite: **North Shore, Blackpool**
The North Pier appears in the distance.

Morning light, near Myerscough
Mist and the low sun broke the landscape into a series
of distinct planes, each more translucent and less solid.

Cottages at Singleton
Outside rush hour, when it's blighted by traffic like everywhere else,
Singleton is a peaceful place with a distinct feeling of yesteryear.

Sandstorm, Bispham
It may seem fanciful to talk of sandstorms in Lancashire, but when I got
down on my knees and elbows to take this shot, it felt quite violent.

Crawley's Dyke
A rare piece of uncultivated land in the Fylde.

The Golden Mile
As hinted in the introduction, 'attractions' are the least of Blackpool's
attractions to me, but it would be perverse to ignore them entirely.

Blowing sand and Lakeland Fells
It's very rare that I wish I could shoot moving images, but this was one
occasion that came close; these streamers of sand swirling along the beach were
a real challenge to capture in a still image.

Frost and mist, near Thistleton
You cannot see great distances in such flat country:
somehow the mist makes it feel bigger.

Opposite: **Rough seas, Blackpool**
A high spring tide and strong onshore wind: to me this is Blackpool at its photographic best.

The shore at Lytham
This is a view south, across the mouth of the Ribble,
to Banks Marsh in West Lancashire.

Opposite: **Rider on Pilling Sands**
The sands seemed to provide an excellent surface for schooling the horse. In the distance a bulk carrier
makes its way out from the port of Heysham and beyond that are the hills of the Furness peninsula.

Fields near Winmarleigh
Around the edge of the Fylde plain the land begins to get a bit more
rumpled. On the horizon are the Bowland Fells.

Opposite: **Evening view from the towpath**
The Lancaster Canal is uninterrupted by locks so its towpath is at a constant elevation
of about 20 metres; quite high enough to open up the views over the Fylde.

Dinghies, Lytham
If these dinghies had all been new and freshly painted
I suspect I'd have found this shot much less appealing.

Opposite: **Old Fire Station, Singleton**
This half-timbered structure originally housed a horse-drawn fire engine. The story
goes that when the alarm was sounded the crew's first job was to catch the horse!
Today, prosaically, it conceals an electricity sub-station.

Spider, Crawley's Dyke
I very nearly blundered through this web without even noticing,
but once I'd got this picture I carefully went around.

Opposite: **Sands, off Rossall Point**
I liked the ripples, picked out by a low sun, but this area is very popular for dog-walking
and it took a few minutes to find a spot where there weren't too many obvious tracks.

Pool Stream
According to the map, the name of this little river is indeed Pool Stream
and there is also a Pool Lane nearby. It flows here into the River Ribble.
In the distance are Winter Hill and the West Pennine moors.

River Wyre
A fine evening by the River Wyre, looking towards the
hill on which Great and Little Eccleston stand.

Façade, Cleveleys
Modern shop-fronts may transform the appearance of buildings
at street level but original features often survive on the upper storeys,
like this Art Deco building on Victoria Road, Cleveleys.

Opposite: **The Lakeland Fells from Cleveleys**
There's snow on the high fells and it was pretty chilly at sea-level too.

Hawthorn berries
The Fylde still retains many miles of hedgerows:
hawthorn is the most characteristic tree.

Blackpool Illuminations
I thought this back view gave a hint of the logistical complexities
of mounting the annual Illuminations.

Milestone, Lancaster Canal
It may be 8 miles from Preston by water,
but it's less than 5 by road from this point.

Opposite: **Harvest, south of Pilling**
This view was taken from the minor road
which runs from Pilling through Eagland Hill.

The Colonnades
The Colonnades along Blackpool's North Shore were completed in 1925.

Blackpool Pleasure Beach
With an annual figure of around 6 million visitors, Blackpool Pleasure Beach is the most popular
attraction in Britain and is reckoned to make the Top Five of amusement parks world-wide.

Grasses, Crawley's Dyke
The uncultivated area alongside Crawley's Dyke
gives clues to the 'natural' vegetation of the Fylde

Opposite: **View to Pilling church**
The spire is that of St John's church, Pilling, a notable landmark. St John's is the
'new' church at Pilling, completed in 1887. The old church still stands nearby.

Union Lane
The general drainage of the mosslands of the Fylde has led to shrinkage, so that roads typically stand above the surrounding fields, and many of the less frequented lanes show obvious signs of subsidence.

Stocks, Poulton-le-Fylde
Behind the stocks is the base of the market cross, and behind that, though
not visible, there is another ancient survivor in the 'fish slab'.

River Brock
The Lancaster Canal crosses over the River Brock by an attractive little
aqueduct, which provided the vantage point for this shot.

River Wyre at Churchtown
St Helen's church at Churchtown (also known as Kirkland) is the original parish church for nearby Garstang and is sometimes referred to as the 'Cathedral of the Fylde'. It is certainly one of the finest churches in the district, with significant parts of its fabric dating back to the thirteenth century.

Dock leaves
On this particular morning I was distracted from shooting broad
landscapes by the luminosity of the foliage at my feet.

Opposite: **Walkers on the beach, St Anne's**
While this shot was taken from the tall dunes north of St Anne's, in fact this scene
could be almost anywhere along the west-facing coast which stretches around
20km from St Anne's to Rossall Point near Fleetwood.

The Mount, Fleetwood
The semi-artificial hill of The Mount was and is a place where families would gather for the first sighting of returning vessels. The pavilion on its summit was built in 1902.

North Wharf, Fleetwood
North Wharf is the name for the extensive area of sand and shoals which
extends several kilometres north from the shoreline at Fleetwood.

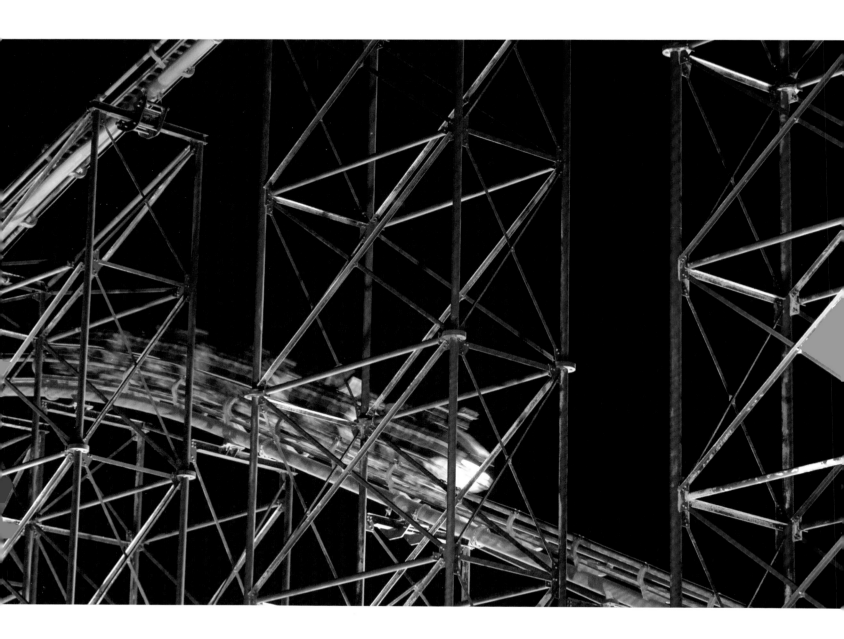

Constabulary Station
This handsome emblem is on the wall of a building
(now a private house) in Great Eccleston.

Opposite: **Roller-coaster**
I was rather preoccupied at the time with the technical challenge of getting any
kind of shot in such low light. It only occurred to me later to wonder whether a
nocturnal ride would be more or less scary than in the daytime.

Drain, off Whitters Lane
The Fylde is criss-crossed with drains and dotted with pumping stations; without them the land would soon revert to its natural swampy condition.

Opposite: **Sheep on Pilling Moss**
The Fylde is overwhelmingly agricultural, with a pretty diverse mix of arable and pastoral farming.

Pharos Lighthouse, Fleetwood
Designed by Decimus Burton, Fleetwood's
principal architect, the Pharos Lighthouse
stands about 25 metres tall.

Pebble in breakwater, Rossall
This pebble was firmly lodged – evidence of the power of the waves. It is a pinkish granite, which must have originated somewhere in the Lake District, or even Scotland.

Stanley Park, Blackpool
Stanley Park lies a couple of kilometres inland. It was laid out in the 1920s and is currently the focus of a major regeneration plan.

Cows, near Inskip
I wanted a shot of the cows grazing with the distant Bowland Fells behind,
but they were so curious that they immediately gave up feeding and all
crowded round, and I had to move the camera before it got licked.

Illuminated tram
While any of Blackpool's trams provide an excellent way to view the Illuminations,
a couple of them are decked with lights to form part of the spectacle.

Opposite: **Cyclist, North Shore**
There is about 15km of continuous promenade from South Shore to Fleetwood, which is
ideal for cycling. The North Shore Colonnades are one of the most notable features.

Wave and Blackpool Tower
I could frame the shot carefully and press the button at the right moment, but I can't take any credit for the prefect form of this wave.

Derelict, Skippool Creek
There's a real irony in the name of this vessel – Good Hope.

Cyclist and breaking wave
This rider may appear to be taking a risk but as a sea angler one
hopes he would know a thing or two about the waves.

Dogs on the beach, Cleveleys
Without doubt, these two setters were having as much fun in
the waves as any of Blackpool's holidaymakers do.

Welcome Home
It's said that it was considered bad luck to
wave goodbye to departing trawlers; this
statue is firmly titled 'Welcome Home'.

THE ASSIGNMENT

BASED ON THE MOTION PICTURE SCREENPLAY 'TOMBOY'.

STORY & SCREENPLAY BY
WALTER HILL &
DENIS HAMILL

ADAPTED BY
MATZ

ART BY
JEF

TRANSLATED BY
CHARLES ARDAI

THE ASSIGNMENT

9781785861451
Published by Titan Comics
A division of Titan Publishing Group Ltd.
144 Southwark St.
London, SE1 0UP

BASED ON THE MOTION PICTURE SCREENPLAY 'TOMBOY'
by Walter Hill & Denis Hamill

Original title: *Corps et âme*
© Rue de Sèvres , Paris, 2017

A CIP catalogue record for this title is available from the British Library

First edition: MARCH 2017

10 9 8 7 6 5 4 3 2 1

Printed in Spain
Titan Comics. 2340

TITAN COMICS

Editor Tom Williams
Senior Designer Andrew Leung

Senior Editor Andrew James
Titan Comics Editorial Jess Burton, Amoona Saohin
Art Director Oz Browne
Production Supervisors Jackie Flook, Maria Pearson
Production Assistant Peter James
Production Manager Obi Onuora
Senior Sales Manager Steve Tothill
Press Officer Will O'Mullane
Marketing Manager Ricky Claydon
Advertising Manager Michelle Fairlamb
Publishing Manager Darryl Tothill
Publishing Director Chris Teather
Operations Director Leigh Baulch
Executive Director Vivian Cheung
Publisher Nick Landau

WWW.TITAN-COMICS.COM

Follow us on Twitter @ComicsTitan
Visit us at facebook.com/comicstitan

WWW.TITAN-COMICS.COM
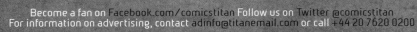
Become a fan on Facebook.com/comicstitan Follow us on Twitter @comicstitan
For information on advertising, contact adinfo@titanemail.com or call +44 20 7620 0200

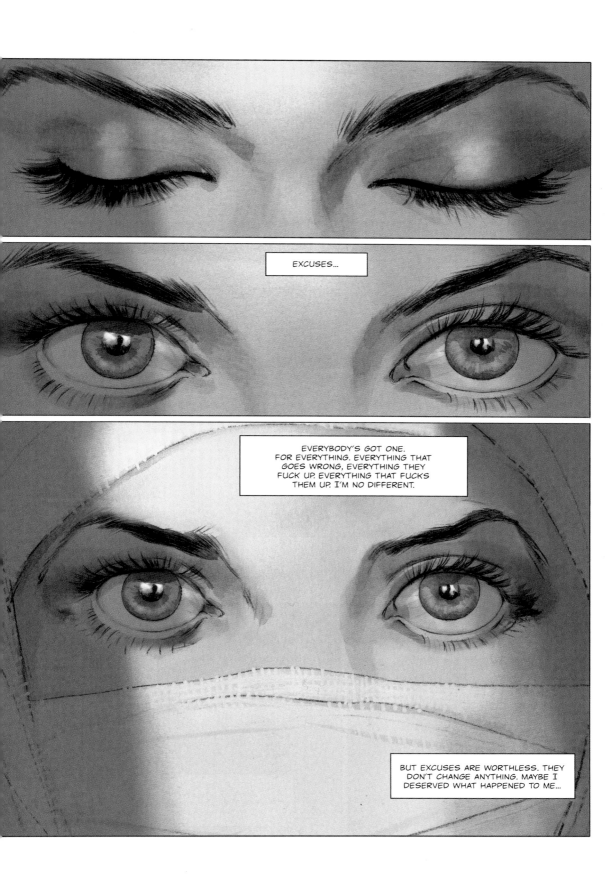

EXCUSES...

EVERYBODY'S GOT ONE.
FOR EVERYTHING. EVERYTHING THAT
GOES WRONG, EVERYTHING THEY
FUCK UP. EVERYTHING THAT FUCKS
THEM UP. I'M NO DIFFERENT.

BUT EXCUSES ARE WORTHLESS. THEY
DON'T CHANGE ANYTHING. MAYBE I
DESERVED WHAT HAPPENED TO ME...

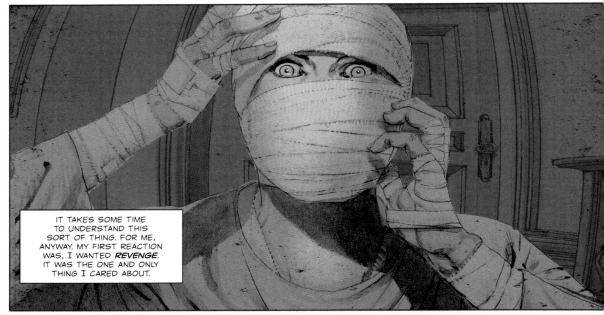

IT TAKES SOME TIME
TO UNDERSTAND THIS
SORT OF THING. FOR ME,
ANYWAY. MY FIRST REACTION
WAS, I WANTED *REVENGE*.
IT WAS THE ONE AND ONLY
THING I CARED ABOUT.

THAT SOMEBODY MIGHT WANT REVENGE
AGAINST *ME*, THAT WAS PREDICTABLE. THAT
THEY MIGHT SUCCEED – THAT TOO. NOTHING
SURPRISING, JUST PART OF THE GAME. YOU
KNOW YOU MIGHT GET TAKEN OUT...

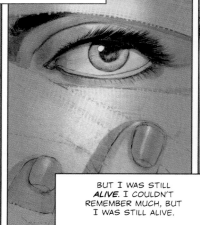

BUT I WAS STILL
ALIVE. I COULDN'T
REMEMBER MUCH, BUT
I WAS STILL ALIVE.

A FEW MONTHS
EARLIER, NEW YORK...

I REMEMBER, IT **WAS FASHION WEEK** IN MANHATTAN.

NOT THE **WORST** ASSIGNMENT I'D EVER HAD.

BUT I WASN'T THERE TO ENJOY THE VIEW. I WAS THERE ON BUSINESS. TO SEE A GUY WHO'D BEEN VERY SUCCESFUL, BUT WHO WASN'T VERY SMART.

SEBASTIAN KAYE. FORMER MODEL, NOW DESIGNER.

A BIG STAR IN HIS FIELD.

RENOWNED THE WORLD OVER - IN MILAN, LONDON, TOKYO, PARIS, L.A., NEW YORK...

A BOY WONDER, IT SEEMED.

THE ULTIMATE IN FASHION AND LUXURY, THE HEIGHT OF TASTE AND SOPHISTICATION.

AREA 51
RESTRICTED ARE
NO TRESSPAS
BEYOND THIS
POINT
GRAPHY

THANK YOU, GIRLS. YOU WERE PERFECT!

I'D DONE MY RESEARCH.

EXCUSE ME.

I'D READ A LOT, BUT IT'S FUNNY, THERE ARE LOTS OF THINGS THE NEWS-PAPERS DON'T TELL YOU. MAYBE THEY DON'T KNOW.

SOMETIMES THOSE THINGS ARE IMPORTANT.

SNïïïïïRRFFFFF

SOMETIMES THEY'RE THINGS THAT COULD COST YOU YOUR LIFE.

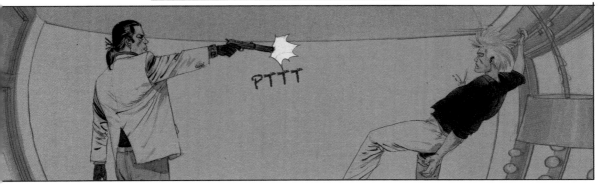

IT'S WHAT I DO. I KILL PEOPLE. WHACK THEM. ICE THEM. MURDER THEM. CALL IT WHAT YOU WILL.

I KNOW IT'S NOT THE SORT OF THING DECENT PEOPLE DO.

IT'S AGAINST EVERY LAW THERE IS - THE LAWS OF GOD AND MAN. IT'S NOT THE WAY THINGS SHOULD BE.

SLAM!

I KNEW AT ONE POINT OR ANOTHER, I'D HAVE TO PAY. I'D ALWAYS KNOWN.

THREE WEEKS
LATER.

ME NEITHER. I'LL PAY FOR THE WEEK UP FRONT. I DON'T WANT TO BE BOTHERED UNDER ANY CIRCUMSTANCE.

WHEN I NEED A MAID, I'LL LET YOU KNOW. UNDERSTAND?

NO PROBLEM. ROOM 302, THIRD FLOOR, A NICE VIEW OF THE STREET. WELCOME TO THE SHANGHAI HOTEL.

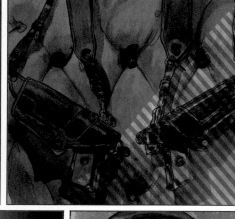

PSHHH

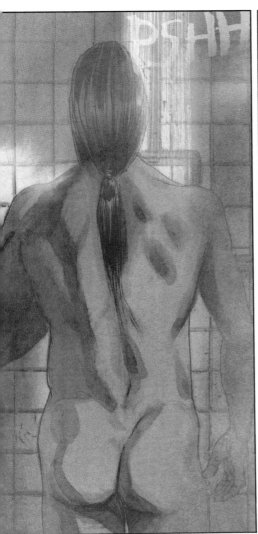

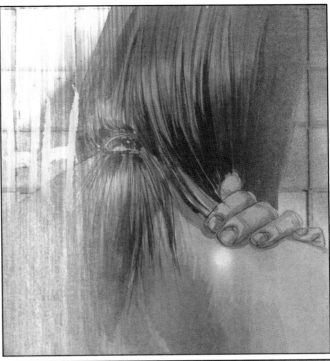

IT'S GOOD TO SEE YOU AGAIN, FRANK. HOW LONG HAS IT BEEN...? TWO YEARS SINCE THE LAST JOB?

SOMETHING LIKE THAT, GLEASON. BUT WHO'S COUNTING?

HA! YOU'RE RIGHT, FRANK. YOU SEE, JIN TAO? FRANK'S A REAL PRO. WE'VE KNOWN EACH OTHER A LONG TIME, BUT NO CHITCHAT. RIGHT TO THE POINT.

HE STOLE SOME MONEY FROM ME. A LOT OF MONEY. AND NOW HE'S TRYING TO STEAL MY BUISINESS. THIS IS A MAN I TRUSTED FOR YEARS. LIKE A BROTHER. I HELPED HIM. I **MADE** HIM. HE OWES EVERYTHING TO ME. AND NOW? HE WANTS TO KLL ME. YOU UNDERSTAND WHY THIS IS SO IMPORTANT TO ME?

CHOW'S GOT BODYGUARDS, LOTS OF THEM. IT WON'T BE EASY TO GET CLOSE TO HIM.

YOU SUPPLY THE NAME. THE REST IS **MY** PROBLEM.

ONE MORE THING, FRANK--

I JUST LEARNED HE'S LEAVING FOR VEGAS TOMORROW. I'VE PROMISED SOME PEOPLE I WOULDN'T MAKE ANY TROUBLE THERE. SO YOU'LL HAVE TO WAIT UNTIL HE'S BACK. ONE WEEK, TOPS.

NO PROBLEM. I CAN DO IT HERE.

YOU SEE THAT, JIN TAO? FRANK'S A MAN WHO KNOWS THE SCORE. HE PLAYS BY THE RULES. YOU GET HALF UP FRONT, FRANK, THE REST WHEN THE JOB IS DONE. JIN TAO?

23

TWENTY-FIVE THOUSAND DOLLARS. TEN IN THOUSANDS, THE REST IN HUNDREDS. TAKES LESS SPACE THIS WAY.

THAT'S ALMOST *DOUBLE* WHAT YOU USUALLY PAY, JOHN.

LIKE I SAID, THIS ONE'S IMPORTANT TO ME.

I THINK YOU'VE MADE YOUR POINT.

"THAT'S GREAT, FRANK. I'LL BE WAITING TO HEAR SOME GOOD NEWS FROM YOU."

"YOU CAN GET THE SECOND HALF OF THE PAYMENT READY."

WHEN YOU COME INTO A PILE OF CASH, YOU'VE GOT A COUPLE OF OPTIONS. YOU CAN KEEP IT ON YOU, BUT THAT'S NOT THE BEST IDEA.

YOU CAN PUT IT IN THE BANK, BUT THAT CAN DRAW ATTENTION, AND YOU MIGHT HAVE TROUBLE GETTING IT BACK.

YOU CAN KEEP IT AT HOME, BUT YOU CAN'T BE SURE YOU WON'T GET AN UNFRIENDLY VISIT SOME-TIME WHEN YOU'RE OUT.

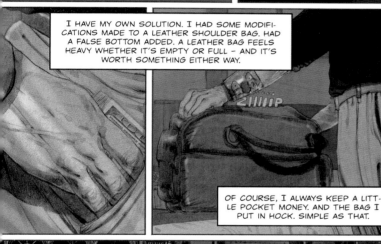

I HAVE MY OWN SOLUTION. I HAD SOME MODIFI-CATIONS MADE TO A LEATHER SHOULDER BAG. HAD A FALSE BOTTOM ADDED. A LEATHER BAG FEELS HEAVY WHETHER IT'S EMPTY OR FULL — AND IT'S WORTH SOMETHING EITHER WAY.

OF COURSE, I ALWAYS KEEP A LITT-LE POCKET MONEY. AND THE BAG I PUT IN HOCK. SIMPLE AS THAT.

UP TILL NOW, IT'S WORKED FOR ME.

PAWN SHOP

WE BUY GOLD

GOLD

THE BAG. IT'S LEATHER. HOW MUCH?

IT'S NICE LEATHER. GOOD CONDITION. I'LL GIVE YOU 25 DOLLARS.

OKAY. YOU'LL HOLD IT HOW LONG?

TWO MONTHS - THAT WORK FOR YOU?

THAT'S FINE. IF I'M NOT BACK FOR IT IN TWO MONTHS, YOU'LL SELL IT?

YOU GOT IT. THAT'S HOW IT WORKS.

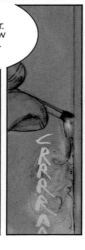

CRRRRA

I HAD NOTHING TO DO BUT KILL TIME, SINCE I COULDN'T KILL ROBERT CHOW. A VACATION OF SORTS. MAYBE IT WOULD DO ME GOOD.

OF COURSE, I'D RATHER HAVE BEEN ON THE COAST IN SAN DIEGO, LYING ON THE BEACH, GETTING SOME SUN. OR IN MEXICO, CATCHING SWORD-FISH. BUT THIS WASN'T SO BAD.

WHISKEY. A DOUBLE. NO ICE.

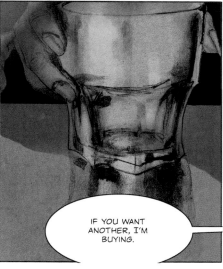

IF YOU WANT ANOTHER, I'M BUYING.

29

THIS IS GOING TO COST ME HOW MUCH?

NOTHING AT ALL. IT'S YOUR LUCKY DAY. I'M NOT A PRO, BUT I DON'T WANT TO SPEND HOURS CHITCHATTING, YOU GET ME?

YOU DON'T LIKE TO TALK?

I HATE THE PEOPLE I WORK FOR. I HATE MY EX. AND THERE'S A LONG LIST OF OTHER PEOPLE IN MY LIFE I'M NOT SUPER HAPPY WITH, SEE?

SO I WOULD REALLY LIKE TO THINK ABOUT SOMETHING ELSE FOR A FEW HOURS WITH SOMEONE LIKE YOU. THAT'S ALL.

IT WAS GOOD, AND I LIKE YOU JUST FINE, BUT DON'T GET ANY IDEAS, OKAY? DON'T EXPECT TO SEE ME AGAIN.

I WAS JUST IN THE RIGHT PLACE AT THE RIGHT TIME, HUH?

SOMETHING LIKE THAT.

DELIGHTED TO HAVE MET YOU, IN ANY CASE.

IF YOU'D LIKE, I'LL BUY YOU A COFFEE.

I THOUGHT I TOLD YOU NOT TO GET ANY IDEAS?

A COFFEE IS NOT AN IDEA. I'LL BE HAVING ONE ACROSS THE STREET IF YOU CARE TO JOIN ME.

THAT'S JUST MACHO BULLSHIT. IF A GIRL GETS CLINGY, YOU TAKE OFF RUNNING. BUT IF SHE TELLS YOU TO TAKE A HIKE, YOU GET INTRIGUED. TELL ME I'M WRONG?

HIDING A BULLET UNDER MY SHOE.

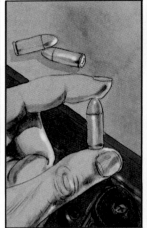

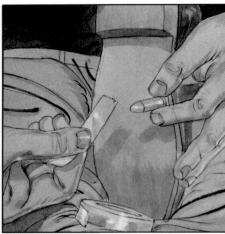

IT'S AN OLD TRICK.

KLIK

KLAK

KNOCK KNOCK

BUT I ALWAYS DO IT. IT CAN SAVE YOUR LIFE.

HELLO, FRANK.

JIN TAO? GLEASON'S NOT COMING? HE LETS YOU OUT ALL BY YOURSELF?

IS THERE A PROBLEM, FRANK?

YEAH. YOU. I DON'T LIKE YOUR MANNERS, JIN TAO. JUST BECAUSE YOU'RE GLEASON'S LITTLE PET DOESN'T MEAN YOU CAN PUSH ME AROUND.

DIDN'T KNOW YOU WERE SO SENSITIVE, FRANK. YOU KNOW I JUST FOLLOW ORDERS.

AND CAN YOU GUESS WHAT MY ORDERS ARE THIS TIME?

GO AHEAD.

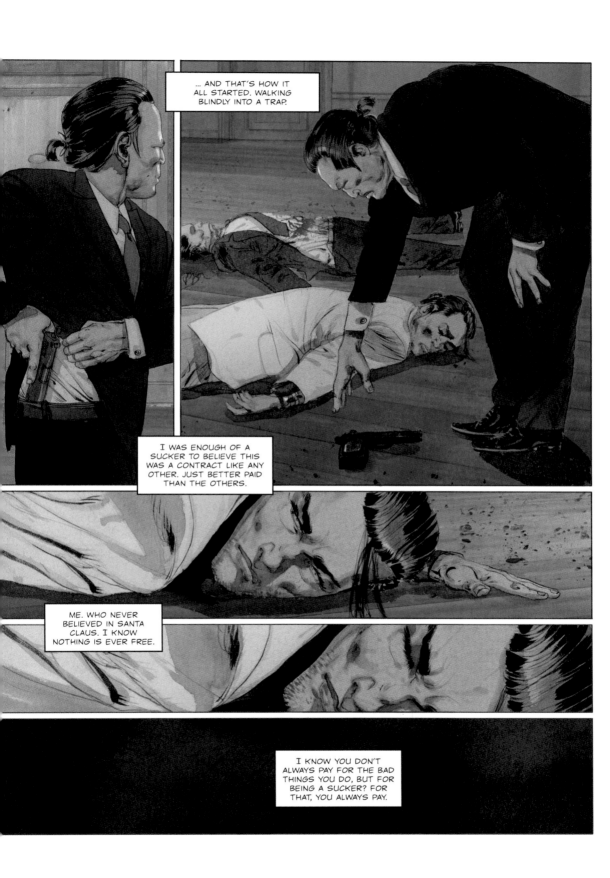

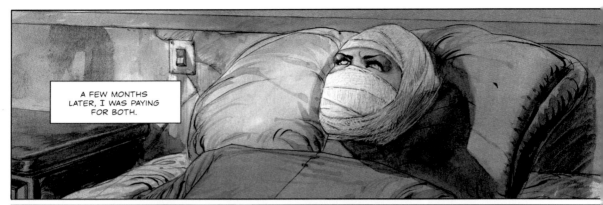

A FEW MONTHS
LATER, I WAS PAYING
FOR BOTH.

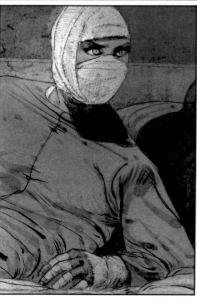

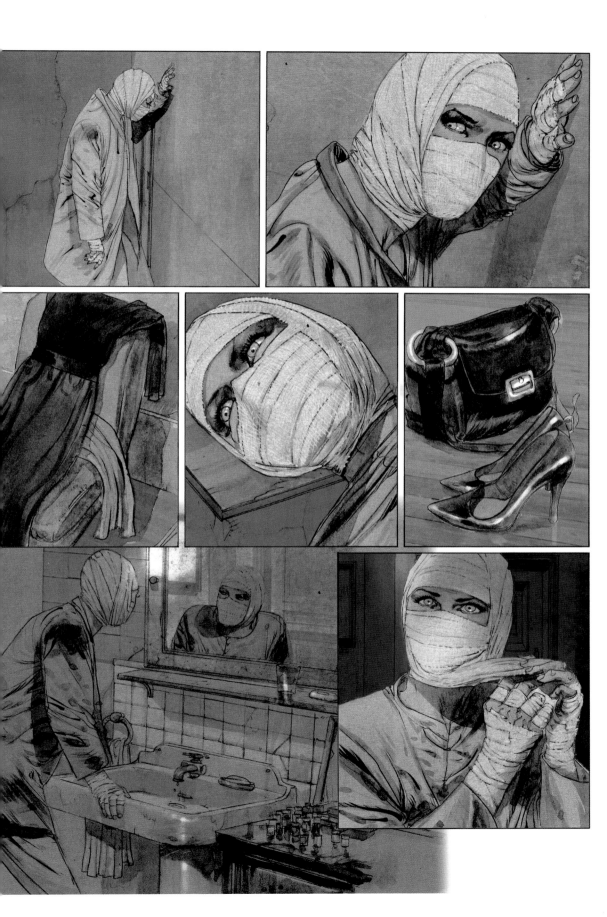

MY
GOD!

44

EXCEPT THAT, ACCORDING TO YOUR FILE, YOU COMMITTED OTHER KILLINGS, OTHER CRIMES, HORRIBLE MUTILATIONS, LONG BEFORE YOUR BROTHER WAS MURDERED. THAT FACT HASN'T ESCAPED YOU, NOT WITH YOUR GENIUS-LEVEL I.Q., HAS IT?

ARE YOU MAKING FUN OF ME? WHAT DO YOU KNOW OF MY I.Q.?

SOME OF THE EXPERTS SAY IT'S OVER 170. SOME SAY THE OPPOSITE. THEY ALL SAY YOU HAVE MEGALOMANIACAL TENDENCIES AND A TENUOUS CONNECTION WITH REALITY. THE HALLMARKS OF A NARCISSISTIC PERSONALITY DISORDER.

IN OTHER WORDS, YOU THINK I'M MAD AS A HATTER. AS EVIDENCED BY THIS RIDICULOUS CAGE YOU HAVE ME IN. YOU CAN GO FUCK YOURSELF.

LET'S TRY SOMETHING ELSE. WHAT CAN YOU TELL ME ABOUT *FRANK KITCHEN*?

THAT HE'S AN ANIMAL. A THUG. A KILLER. NOTHING MORE. BUT I *RE-MADE* HIM.

GET OUT OF HERE!

CALM DOWN, LADY! I HEARD SCREAMING AND CAME TO SEE WHAT WAS GOING ON. THOUGHT MAYBE YOU WERE HAVING PROBLEMS.

I HAVE EVERY RIGHT TO BE HERE. I'M THE LANDLORD. AND HEY, I LIKE YOUR *VOICE* - VERY SEXY. WHAT'RE YOU DOING HERE ANYWAY? THE ROOM WAS RENTED BY TWO GUYS, NOT A GIRL...

WHAT WERE THEY LIKE, THESE GUYS?

BIG GUYS. NOT THE SUIT-AND-TIE-TYPE. THEY PAID A MONTH UP FRONT, CASH. NEVER SAW THEM AGAIN.

ANYWAY, DON'T MAKE SUCH A RACKET. OKAY, CUTIE? I LIKE YOUR *TOMBOY* STYLE AND ALL, BUT I RUN A RESPECTABLE PLACE. THIS AIN'T NO *WHOREHOUSE*. DO I MAKE MYSELF CLEAR?

BUT YOU WILL HAVE TO MAINTAIN YOUR NEW FEMININITY WITH HORMONES — IF YOU DON'T, YOU'LL WIND UP A CIRCUS FREAK. I'VE PREPARED EVERYTHING FOR YOU. FOLLOW THE INSTRUCTIONS AND ALL WILL BE WELL.

IT WAS A LOT TO TAKE IN. IT TOOK SOME TIME BEFORE I COULD PROCESS WHAT HAD BEEN DONE TO ME IN A COHERENT AND LOGICAL MANNER.

AT FIRST, IT MADE ME INSANE. *COMPLETELY* INSANE.

I DON'T NEED YOUR GODDAMN PILLS...

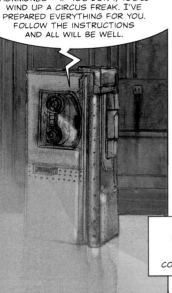

NO, WHAT I REALLY NEEDED WAS A DRINK. HELL — I NEEDED THE WHOLE BOTTLE. BUT IT TOOK ME THREE DAYS TO WORK UP THE COURAGE TO LEAVE THE ROOM.

LIQUOR

Gratiot
LIQUOR
BEER WINE
LOTTO
Money Orders

Gratiot
LIQUOR
BEER WINE LOTTO ATM MONEY ORDER

Gratiot
LIQUOR
BEER WINE LOTTO MONEY ORDER

WE ACCEPT
BRIDGE CARD
EBT
AT BLUE STORE
LIQUOR
PRICES
STATE MINIMUM

WE ACC
BRIDGE
E B
AT BLU
LIQ
PRIC
STAT

THERE HAD BEEN BAD TIMES IN MY LIFE, TIMES WHEN I NEEDED A BOOST, BUT NONE LIKE THIS. I REALIZED I MUST'VE SPENT WEEKS UNCONSCIOUS – MAYBE *MONTHS* - AFTER BEING BUTCHERED AND BEFORE WAKING UP IN THIS CRUMMY HOTEL.

MY HEAD STILL WASN'T ENTIRELY CLEAR – AND THE VODKA WASN'T HELPING. BUT I KNEW TWO THINGS...

FIRST: I HAD TO GET THE FUCK OUT OF HERE.

SECOND: I'D NEED MONEY IN ORDER TO DO SO.

ANYWAY, IT'S NEVER A GOOD IDEA TO LEAVE CASH LYING AROUND UNGUARDED.

ESPECIALLY WITH A GUY LIKE *ME* ON THE PREMISES.

EVEN IF I WASN'T ENTIRELY SURE YOU COULD REALLY CALL ME A *GUY* ANYMORE.

HEY! WHAT ARE YOU...

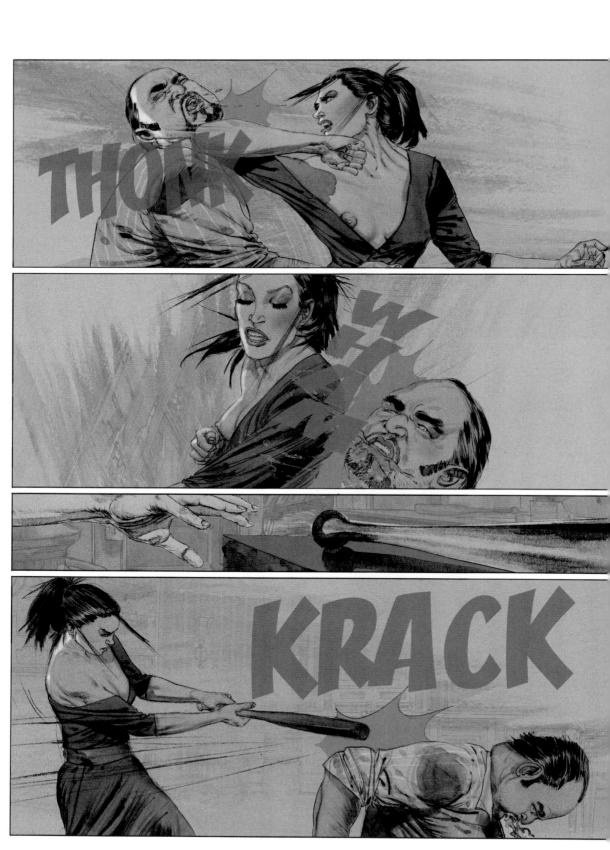

CRASH

IT CAME OVER ME, THE NEED TO **SMASH**, TO **BREAK** SOMETHING. I FELT A LOT BETTER NOW.

MAYBE THE GUY WAS DEAD. MAYBE NOT. I DIDN'T CHECK. I DIDN'T GIVE A FUCK.

HE'D BEEN ASKING FOR IT. IF HE CAME TO, HE WOULDN'T CALL THE COPS. AND IF HE NEVER WOKE UP, THAT WOULD JUST BE ONE LESS PIECE OF SHIT ON THE PLANET.

I HAD LITTLE MORE THAN 500 DOLLARS AND NOWHERE TO GO. BUT NOT HAVING ANYWHERE TO GO WASN'T GOING TO STOP ME FROM GETTING THE FUCK OUT.

I HAD THE CASH FROM THE REGISTER, THE DRUGS, AND THAT WAS IT.

AND THIS *PHOTO*, WHICH HAD BEEN WITH THE DRUGS. I REMEMBERED THE GUY.

IT WAS THAT ARROGANT PRICK FROM THE FASHION SHOW IN NEW YORK. THE ONE WHO BORROWED MONEY FROM PEOPLE YOU DON'T FUCK WITH.

AFTER THAT, I'D BEEN HIRED BY THE GUYS IN MIAMI. I'D DONE A GOOD JOB. IF THEY WEREN'T HAPPY OR THOUGHT I KNEW TOO MUCH, THEY COULD'VE JUST BUMPED ME OFF. THEY SURE WEREN'T BEHIND THIS.

I DIDN'T UNDERSTAND IT. I DIDN'T UNDERSTAND ANYTHING..

NONE OF IT MADE SENSE, WHICH TOLD ME ONE THING: I WAS DEALING WITH SOMEONE WHO *WASN'T* PART OF THE UNDERWORLD...

LAST, STOP MY DEAR. YOU'LL HAVE TO GET OFF.

I NEEDED TO PUT SOME DISTANCE BETWEEN ALL THAT AND ME. MY CONTRACTS. MY EMPLOYERS, MY JOB, THE PAST.

I THINK I MUST HAVE BEEN *DEPRESSED* OR SOMETHING, LIKE A SOLDIER WHEN HE RETURNS FROM THE FRONT.

IT WOULD TAKE ME SOME TIME TO GET BACK ON MY FEET.

HEY, BITCH, THIS IS *MY* SPOT.

WE DON'T WANT ANYONE ELSE HERE. THERE AIN'T ENOUGH EATS TO GO 'ROUND.

I'M FATHER PATRICK. I CAN OFFER YOU A BED AND SOMETHING TO EAT. JUST ONE RULE HERE: NO ALCOHOL.

THANK YOU. WHAT I REALLY WANT IS TO EARN MY KEEP.

I CAN FND YOU WORK THAT PAYS 20 DOLLARS A DAY.

IN CASH?

IN CASH. YOU'RE STILL YOUNG. YOU CAN MAKE A FRESH START. IT WOULD BE NICE, FOR ONCE, TO SEE SOMEONE DO BETTER.

BUT REMEMBER, THIS OFFER ONLY STANDS IF YOU DON'T DRINK.

AGREED. I'LL DO MY BEST, FATHER.

EVERYONE SAYS 'AGREED' - BUT EVERY DAY, I FIND EMPTY BOTTLES ON THE FLOOR OF THE DORM OR IN THE TRASH BINS. IF YOU BREAK THE RULE, I'LL PUT YOU RIGHT BACK OUT. YOU'VE BEEN WARNED.

ASSUMING FOR NOW THAT THIS 'FRANK KITCHEN' ACTUALLY EXISTS, WHY DO YOU HATE HIM SO MUCH?

WHY WOULDN'T HE EXIST? YOU THINK I MADE HIM UP?

YOU'RE CERTAINLY CAPABLE OF IT. TO HIDE SOMETHING EVEN WORSE THAT YOU MIGHT HAVE DONE, FOR EXAMPLE. TAKE IT AS A CREDIT TO THE INTELLIGENCE YOU'RE SO PROUD OF AND ANSWER THE QUESTION: WHY DO YOU HATE HIM SO MUCH?

ISN'T IT OBVIOUS? HE KILLED SEBASTIAN.

BUT HE WAS JUST A HIRED GUN. IF WHAT YOU SAY IS TRUE, SHOULDN'T YOU HATE THE MAN WHO *HIRED* HIM? WHY NOT GO AFTER HIM?

EASIER SAID THAN DONE! THE MAN WHO GAVE THE ORDER IS HIGH UP IN A CRIMINAL ORGANIZATION – THE KIND OF MAN WHOSE ENEMIES HAVE A VERY *SHORT* LIFE EXPECTANCY.

SO YOU WENT AFTER THE WEAK LINK?

YOU CAN LOOK AT IT THAT WAY, I SUPPOSE. BUT YOU CAN ALSO LOOK AT IT FROM A DIFFERENT ANGLE. SEBASTIAN OWED A LOT OF MONEY TO THIS MAN. HE KNEW THE RISKS BUT HE DIDN'T PAY...

SEBASTIAN WAS A SPECIAL SOUL. HE WAS SMART, HANDSOME, TALENTED, FUNNY, SOPHISTICATED. BUT HE WAS ALSO A FOOL WHO IGNORED THE CONSEQUENCES OF HIS ACTIONS. HE THOUGHT HE WAS UNTOUCHABLE, INVULNERABLE, ABOVE IT ALL...

IF IT WAS A QUESTION OF MONEY, GIVEN HOW RICH YOU ARE, WHY DIDN'T YOU PAY HIS DEBTS?

I DID! I GAVE HIM ENOUGH TO PAY THEM OFF – BUT HE SPENT IT ALL AND NEVER TOLD ME. THAT'S HOW HE WAS.

AND FRANK KITCHEN?

I'M TORN. ON ONE HAND I THINK HE'S *FILTH*, LIKE A POACHER WHO KILLS ELEPHANTS FOR THEIR TUSKS, OR THE AUSCHWITZ GUARD WHO SENDS PEOPLE TO DEATH WITHOUT BATTING AN EYELID. A BRUTE WHO THINKS OF NOTHING BUT MONEY, WITH NO CONSCIENCE...

ON THE OTHER HAND, IN SOME WAYS, HE'S *ADMIRABLE*. HE HAS COURAGE, HE'S PREPARED TO KILL AND TO DIE, THERE'S NO FEAR IN HIM. IT DIDN'T STOP ME FROM WANTING TO MAKE HIM PAY. BUT PERHAPS HE COULD BE USEFUL.

SAY WHAT YOU WILL, BUT FATHER PATRICK SAVED ME. THANKS TO HIM, I GOT BACK ON TRACK. THE JOBS WEREN'T GLAMOROUS, BUT THEY HELPED ME GET MY HEAD ON STRAIGHT.

BUT I HADN'T KEPT MY WORD. EACH WEEK, I SET ASIDE PART OF MY PAY; THE REST, I *DRANK*.

CIGARS
LIQUORS
BEER·WINE
WOERNER'S CIGARS LIQUORS

WHISKEY, RUM, VODKA – DIDN'T MATTER WHICH.

HERE'S WHERE WE ARE, DR. FELLNER: A WEALTHY PLASTIC SURGEON COMPLETELY LOSES HER MARBLES, AND STARTS PERFORMING *EXPERIMENTS* – AMPUTATIONS – ON MEN CHOSEN AT RANDOM, GENERALLY HOMELESS MEN PICKED UP ON THE STREET. SPECIALIZING IN *SEX CHANGE* SURGERY.

MOST OF THE TIME, THE VICTIMS *DIE* IN THE OPERATING ROOM. THE ONES THAT SURVIVE TO LODGE A COMPLAINT, NO ONE BELIEVES.

THIS WOMAN IS A MONSTER LIKE NOTHING I'VE EVER SEEN. WE DON'T HAVE ANY IDEA HOW MANY VICTIMS THERE WERE?

SHE DOESN'T WANT TO SAY. SHE WON'T TALK ABOUT ANYONE BUT THIS FRANK KITCHEN. SHE'S OBSESSED WITH HIM, AND WE DON'T EVEN KNOW IF HE'S REAL. THE FBI HAS NOTHING ON HIM. IF HE DOES EXIST, IT'S UNDER ANOTHER NAME.

IT DOESN'T HELP THAT WE'VE ALSO FAILED TO TURN UP THIS NURSE SHE'S MENTIONED. IF WE COULD, SHE MIGHT BE ABLE TO TELL US A THING OR TWO.

I'LL TRY TO FIND OUT MORE, BUT IT ISN'T EASY TO GET HER TO TALK. JUST BEING IN THE SAME ROOM WITH HER IS CREEPY, BELIEVE ME.

HI THERE. YOU LOOKING FOR SOME COMPANY?

NO, THANKS.

YOU'RE ONLY SAYING THAT BECAUSE YOU DON'T KNOW US YET, MY BUDDY TOM AND ME.

IF YOU ASK ME, YOU'RE WAY TOO HOT TO BE ALONE TONIGHT. AND WE JUST HAPPENED TO BE LOOKING FOR A GIRL LIKE YOU, TO HAVE SOME FUN.

UNLESS MAYBE YOU DON'T LIKE BLACK GUYS?

YOU'LL CHANGE YOUR TUNE, YOU'LL SEE.

HOW ABOUT LEAVING ME ALONE?

HA! HA! HA!

JEEZ, DON'T TAKE IT LIKE THAT, IT'S JUST A JOKE – WHAT? COME BACK AND HAVE A DRINK.

NOT LONG AGO, I WOULD'VE SHOWN THOSE TWO SHITHEELS WHAT IT'S LIKE TO FIND THEMSELVES AT THE WRONG END OF A .45, BUT THE LAST THING I NEEDED RIGHT NOW WAS TROUBLE WITH THE POLICE.

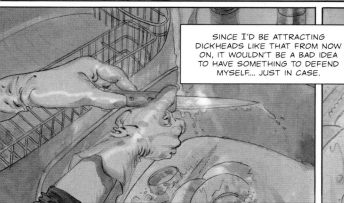

SINCE I'D BE ATTRACTING DICKHEADS LIKE THAT FROM NOW ON, IT WOULDN'T BE A BAD IDEA TO HAVE SOMETHING TO DEFEND MYSELF.... JUST IN CASE.

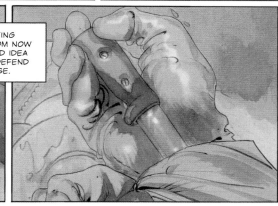

WHICH PROVED MY PRIMAL INSTINCTS WERE BACK IN ORDER.

A FEW DAYS LATER...

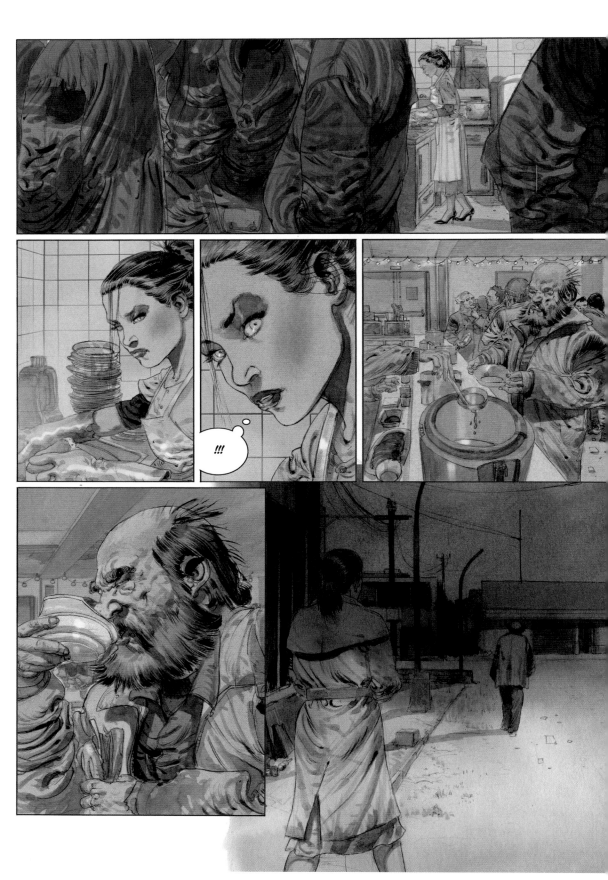

IT WASN'T WORTH THE TROUBLE OF KILLING HIM. HE'D EVEN DONE ME A FAVOR: THANKS TO HIM, I KNEW WHO I WAS AGAIN AND WHAT I HAD TO DO.

I LEFT THE MISSION. FATHER PATRICK HAD SAVED MY LIFE FOR SURE, AND I WAS PROFOUNDLY GRATEFUL...

BUT RIGHT NOW, I HAD THINGS TO DO. SCORES TO SETTLE.

TO START WITH, I HAD TO FIND CLOTHING WORTHY OF THE NEW ME...

CLOTHES I'D FEEL GOOD IN.

ONES THAT WOULD ALLOW ME TO PASS UNNOTICED, AND ALSO HIDE A FEW SCARS.

I ALSO NEEDED MONEY, A PLACE TO SLEEP, AND A GUN... OR MAYBE TWO. IT WAS ALL PART OF REDISCOVERING MYSELF. IN A NEW BODY, SURE, BUT STILL ME.

FIRST, I NEEDED MY BAG.

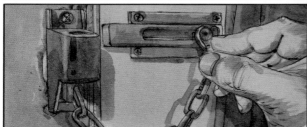

THEY'RE CLEAN. NEVER USED. UNKNOWN TO THE POLICE. YOU UNDERSTAND WHAT I'M SAYING?

ABSOLUTELY. I'LL TAKE THIS .45 WITH THREE MAGAZINES AND AMMO.

CLIK

CLAK

HOW MUCH?

UMM, 650 DOLLARS.

FINE. I'LL ALSO TAKE THIS SMITH AND WESSON WITH A BOX OF BULLETS.

500 MORE. SAY, YOU SEEM TO KNOW A LOT ABOUT FIREARMS, FOR A--

-- WOMAN? YES, I KNOW. $1,000 FOR THE LOT?

DEAL.

I FELT LIKE I WAS BACK IN THE SADDLE AGAIN. I HADN'T BEEN MYSELF FOR A WHILE, BUT THAT WAS OVER. MAN OR WOMAN, SAME DIFFERENCE FOR ME. BUT FOR THE PEOPLE WHO'D DONE THIS TO ME, IT WAS GOING TO CHANGE EVERYTHING.

HELLO? HELLO, MAY I SPEAK WITH *JOHNNIE*?

IT'S FRANK. I'M IN TOWN. WANT TO GET A COFFEE? SAME PLACE? GOOD. TONIGHT.

JOHNNIE !

IS... IS THAT YOU, FRANK?

YOU'RE... DIFFERENT...

YOU DON'T KNOW HOW RIGHT YOU ARE. AND YOU? WHAT ARE YOU UP TO?

I'M STILL A *NURSE*. I NEVER TOLD YOU?

OR MAYBE I ONLY TOLD YOU THAT I HATE MY JOB? I HATE THE PEOPLE I WORK FOR, I TOLD YOU THAT. BUT YOU... WHAT'S HAPPENED TO YOU?

IT'S A LITTLE COMPLICATED.

SO... DISGUISING YOURSELF AS A WOMAN, EH? YOU REALLY PULLED IT OFF, YOU KNOW. WHAT IS IT? YOU HIDING FROM THE COPS?

I WANTED TO CALL YOU...

YOU TOOK YOUR TIME.

I HAD SOME... PROBLEMS.

CLEARLY... I CAN SEE THAT. MAYBE I CAN HELP YOU? IS THAT WHY YOU CALLED ME?

I NEED A PLACE TO STAY, ONE OR TWO WEEKS. I CAN PAY YOU.

I DON'T WANT YOUR MONEY.

I HAVE A SCORE OR TWO TO SETTLE, AND THERE'S SOMETHING ELSE, SOMETHING I SHOULD TELL YOU FIRST.

YOU CAN EXPLAIN IT ALL AT MY PLACE, OKAY?

YOU KNOW, I ALWAYS TRUST MY INTUITION, AND I GET A GOOD VIBE FROM YOU. PEOPLE MIGHT SAY I'M CRAZY, BUT WE'LL SEE. HERE WE ARE – DON'T GET EXCITED, I'M NO MARTHA STEWART.

BUT...

IT... IT'S *NOT* A DISGUISE.

I DON'T UNDERSTAND.

ME EITHER.

HOW IS THAT POSSIBLE?

IT'S A CRAZY THING. I WAS KNOCKED UNCONCIOUS, AND WHEN I CAME TO, I WAS... LIKE *THIS*.

CLIK

BUT... HOW? WHY...?

THAT'S WHAT I'M TRYING TO FIND OUT. I WANT TO GET MY HANDS ON THE PERSON WHO DID THIS TO ME.

AND WHEN YOU'VE FOUND THEM?

IT COULD BECOME *UNHEALTHY.*

LOOKS LIKE IT ALREADY HAS.

I DON'T WANT TO DRAG YOU INTO MY TROUBLES. THERE WILL BE BODIES, AND THE COPS WILL GET INVOLVED FOR SURE.

I LIKE HAVING YOU AROUND. I DON'T WANT YOU TO LEAVE.

OKAY.

SO, WHAT HAPPENS NEXT?

WE GET SOME REST. THERE'LL BE BLOOD SPILLED TOMORROW, AND I DON'T WANT IT TO BE MINE...

FOR SOMEONE LIKE ME, IT'S NOT HARD TO GET MY HANDS ON THE HUMAN GARBAGE THAT WORK UNDER HONEST JOHN GLEASON.

THEY'D BE UP TO THEIR ELBOWS IN ALL THE DIRTY BUSINESS OF THE CITY, AND THAT SORT OF ACTIVITY ALWAYS TAKES PLACE IN THE SAME SPOTS.

I KNEW **WHO** TO ASK, AND I KNEW **HOW** TO ASK.

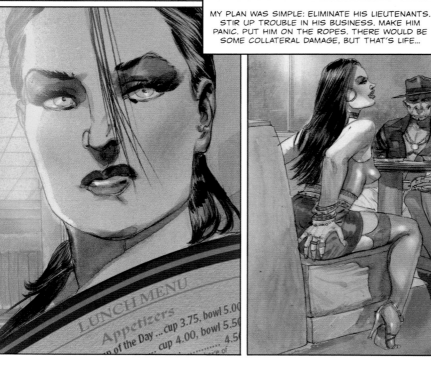

MY PLAN WAS SIMPLE: ELIMINATE HIS LIEUTENANTS. STIR UP TROUBLE IN HIS BUSINESS. MAKE HIM PANIC. PUT HIM ON THE ROPES. THERE WOULD BE SOME COLLATERAL DAMAGE, BUT THAT'S LIFE...

EARL HAWKINS.
HONEST JOHN'S HEAD
PIMP. FROM WHAT I'D
HEARD, IF A GIRL GOT
OUT OF LINE, HE
LOVED CORRECTING
HER HIMSELF. PUTTING
THEM THROUGH HELL
WAS HIS PERSONAL
SPECIALTY.

I'M PRETTY SURE I
UNLOADED A WHOLE MAGAZINE
INTO HIS BELLY. CHANCES OF
SURVIVAL: NIL. AND NO RISK
OF A STRAY BULLET KILLING
AN INNOCENT BYSTANDER, IF
SUCH A THING EVEN EXISTS.

BLAM!
BLAM!
BLAM!

AFTER THAT, THERE WERE MORE LIKE HIM. BAGMEN, TRIGGERMEN, RIGHT-HAND MEN. MEMBERS OF AFFILIATED GANGS...

POW! POW! POW!

DON'T SHOOT! JESUS! I'LL TELL YOU ANYTHING YOU WANT TO KNOW, JUST DONT SHOOT!

IN A COUPLE OF WEEKS, I'D THINNED OUT GLEASON'S OPERATION MORE EFFECTIVELY THAN THE POLICE AND THE COURTS HAD IN TEN YEARS.

THANKS TO ME, THE CITY WAS CONSIDERABLY CLEANER, BUT NO ONE WAS GOING TO GIVE ME A MEDAL.

BUT THAT'S OKAY. I HADN'T DONE IT FOR THE SAKE OF JUSTICE. IT WAS TO WEAKEN GLEASON. TO SCARE THE LIVING SHIT OUT OF HIM.

TARIK PURIFOY. IN CHARGE OF LOANSHARKING. HIS HOBBY: TRAINING DOGS AND MAKING THEM FIGHT. I HEARD HE LIKED ELECTROCUTING THE LOSERS AND WATCHING THEM DIE.

CHARMING GUY. ESPECIALLY FOR ME. I LOVE DOGS. THEY'RE THE ONLY CREATURES I'VE EVER FOUND WORTHY OF MY TRUST. IF YOU'RE RICH, POOR, SMART, DUMB, FAMOUS OR A BUM, A DOG DOESN'T GIVE A DAMN.

GRRRR

WOOF WOOF WOOF

ALL A DOG WANTS IS TO BE YOUR FRIEND. AND THIS SON OF A BITCH LIKED TO FRY THEM FOR FUN, IF THEY LOST HIS GODDAMN FIGHTS.

YOU'RE THE ONE WHO CALLED ABOUT A DOG?

YES. IS THAT HIM THERE?

YEAH. HIS NAME'S *PANCHO*. HE'LL COST YOU $2,000, BUT HE'LL MAKE YOU MORE THAN THAT IN TWO OR THREE FIGHTS.

WOOF

CAN I GO INTO THE CAGE?

IF I PUT A MUZZLE ON HIM FIRST. HE'S A REAL BAD SEED, YOU KNOW? A BORN FIGHTER.

THERE'S NO SUCH THING.

91

ALL I WANTED WAS REVENGE AGAINST THE PIECE OF SHIT WHO'D DONE THIS TO ME, LEFT ME IN THIS CONDITION. AND SOMEHOW I'D WOUND UP WITH A GIRL AND A DOG. MY WHOLE LIFE, I'D AVOIDED DOMESTIC RESPONSIBILITY AND THIS WASN'T THE TIME TO START.

REVENGE WAS STILL MY MAIN GOAL. BUT I ALSO HAD QUESTIONS ONLY A DOCTOR COULD ANSWER. SO I WENT TO ONE. I GOT ANSWERS. BUT NOT THE ONES I'D BEEN HOPING FOR.

IS IT POSSIBLE TO BECOME A MAN AGAIN, DOC?

IT'S NORMAL TO GO THROUGH A PHASE WHERE YOU HAVE DOUBTS, WHERE YOUR FEELINGS OVERWHELM YOU. IT'S VERY COMMON. I CAN RECOMMEND AN EXCELLENT THERAPIST, IF YOU'D LIKE?

I COULD TAKE OUT THE IMPLANTS, OF COURSE. BUT I CAN'T MAKE YOU A MAN AGAIN. WE COULD MAKE YOU... SOMETHING, BUT IT WOULD BE PURELY COSMETIC. NOT FUNCTIONAL, YOU UNDERSTAND? GIVEN THE CURRENT STATE OF MEDICINE, IT'S *IMPOSSIBLE*.

BUT IS WHAT I'M ASKING *POSSIBLE*?

ANOTHER VODKA!

YOU'VE ALREADY HAD A LOT. YOU'RE SURE YOU WANT ANOTHER, HONEY?

WHO ARE YOU, MY *FATHER*?

RIGHT ON! POUR HER ANOTHER, AND GIVE ME ONE TOO. IT'S ON ME.

THANKS.

YOU FOLLOW FOOTBALL?

NO.

WOULDN'T YOU LIKE TO GO SOMEWHERE ELSE, THEN? SOMEWHERE QUIETER?

NO.

I LIVE JUST A COUPLE BLOCKS AWAY. IT'S NICER THAN HERE.

I SAID NO.

COME ON. I'VE GOT BOOZE AT MY PLACE, AND YOU'LL SEE, I'M NO SLOUCH IN THE SACK.

... FINE. LET'S GO

SSHHHHH

IT WAS JUST TOO MUCH. I NEEDED TO TAKE IT OUT ON SOMEONE. I ADMIT, IT WASN'T NICE OF ME, BUT HE'D KIND OF BEEN ASKING FOR IT.

TILL THEN, I'D NEVER REALIZED JUST HOW *AWFUL* SOME GUYS ARE. IT WAS A LESSON FOR ME. IT DID ME GOOD TO LEARN IT.

I'D ELIMINATED SEVERAL GROUPS IN GLEASON'S ORGANIZATION. HE HAD TO BE GETTING ANXIOUS. HE HAD A BUNCH OF FRONTS FOR LAUNDERING MONEY, MAINLY RESTAURANTS – THEY'RE THE BEST FOR IT. PLUS, THAT WAY, HIS MEN GOT FREE MEALS.

ONE OF THE GUYS I'D TAKEN OUT HAD TIPPED ME OFF BEFORE DYING AS TO WHERE I STOOD THE BEST CHANCE OF GETTING THE DROP ON JIN TAO. HE MADE A HABIT OF GOING TO ONE OF GLEASON'S JOINTS BETWEEN 11 AT NIGHT AND 1AM.

WHEN SHOOTING A MAN BY
HIMSELF, A SILENCER IS GOOD.
BUT IF YOU'RE GOING UP AGAINST
AN ARMED GANG, I'D ADVISE YOU
TO LEAVE THE SILENCER AT HOME.
A .45 MAKES A LOT OF NOISE,
AND WHEN MEN ARE SCARED,
THEIR AIM SUFFERS.

DID YOU SEE
HIS FACE WHEN
I TOLD HIM...?

JIN TAO!
MY OLD FRIEND.
HOW ARE YOU
DOING THESE
DAYS?

DO I
KNOW
YOU?

YOU DON'T RECOGNIZE ME?
AND YOU TWO, KEEP YOUR HANDS
WHERE I CAN SEE THEM,
UNDERSTAND?

I THOUGHT
YOU WERE
DEAD. WHAT
HAPPENED
TO YOU?

THAT'S EXACTLY WHAT I
WAS GOING TO ASK YOU.
THAT, AND WHY YOUR
BOSS LAID A TRAP
FOR ME.

THE
ANSWER'S
ALWAYS THE SAME,
YOU KNOW. YOU OUGHTA
KNOW IT BETTER THAN
ANYONE: *MONEY.*

THE BULLET WENT THROUGH. I'LL CLEAN IT AND BANDAGE IT. YOU'LL LIVE.

AAAH!

LOOK AT YOU. DOES BABY WANT A BLANKIE TO HOLD?

THERE. WE'LL CHANGE IT TOMORROW. BUT DON'T CRY ANYMORE, LITTLE GIRL. OKAY? IT HURTS MY EARS.

I'LL DO MY BEST, NURSE. BUT SOMEONE REALLY SHOULD TEACH YOU HOW TO BE GENTLE.

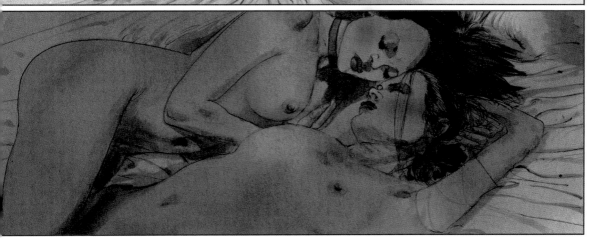

WHAT ARE YOU GOING TO DO NOW?

I'LL GET MY HANDS ON GLEASON AND SETTLE OUR SCORE. BUT FIRST, HE'LL HAVE TO GIVE ME A NAME.

YOU DON'T THINK HE'LL BE ON HIS GUARD? I IMAGINE HE'S PROBABLY GOT A SMALL ARMY AROUND HIM. IT'S WHAT I'D DO IN HIS PLACE...

THAT WON'T STOP SOMEONE FROM TAKING HIM DOWN. YOU KNOW THAT AS WELL AS I DO.

YOU THINK IT'S WORTH IT?

I DON'T THINK I HAVE A CHOICE. HEY - SINCE YOU'RE INVOLVED NOW, I HAVE A QUESTION FOR YOU. WHAT THEY'VE DONE TO ME... WHAT DOES IT *MAKE* ME?

YOU KNOW, FRANK. YOU CAN BE WHATEVER YOU WANT.

GREAT. YOU SOUND LIKE A FUCKING TALK SHOW.

WELL, I GUESS YOU COULD SAY YOU'VE BECOME A LESBIAN.

... SINCE YOU STILL LIKE *GIRLS*. I ENJOYED IT TOO, OF COURSE. MAYBE *I'M* THE LESBIAN?

BETTER. MUCH BETTER.

THERE'S EVEN SOMETHING POSITIVE IN ALL THIS.

OH, YEAH? WHAT?

THE COPS AREN'T LOOKING FOR A *WOMAN*. STAYING FEMALE MIGHT BE YOUR BEST CHANCE OF NOT WINDING UP IN THE SLAMMER. YOU CAN MAKE UP A NEW NAME, A NEW IDENTITY. BECOME SOME- ONE ELSE.

YOU'D WANT ME TO COME WITH YOU?

WITH ME.

OU SHOULD DUMP ME. YOU KNOW OU'RE HARBORING CRIMINAL. IT COULD T YOU TEN YEARS BEHIND BARS.

NOT COUNTING FIVE YEARS OF PROBATION, I KNOW.

I'M READY TO DROP EVERYTHING TO GO WITH YOU. MY MOTHER'S DEAD. MY DAD'S IN NORTH DAKOTA, WHICH AMOUNTS TO THE SAME THING. I DON'T HAVE MANY FRIENDS. NOBODY WILL NOTICE I'M GONE. AND I COULD BE HANDY FROM TIME TO TIME, IF YOU KEEP GETTING SHOT.

TALK TO ME ABOUT *GLEASON*. ACCORDING TO THE POLICE, HE FURNISHED YOU WITH HOMELESS MEN AND TRANSIENTS FOR YOUR SO-CALLED EXPERIMENTS.

GLEASON IS A STRANGE CREATURE: KILL OR BE KILLED, SEIZE MONEY AND POWER BY ANY MEANS NECESSARY. BUT I'M A DOCTOR, A SCIENTIST, SO THERE'S NOTHING I CAN REALLY TELL YOU ABOUT HIM.

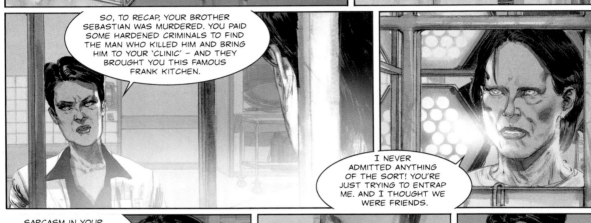

SO, TO RECAP, YOUR BROTHER SEBASTIAN WAS MURDERED. YOU PAID SOME HARDENED CRIMINALS TO FIND THE MAN WHO KILLED HIM AND BRING HIM TO YOUR 'CLINIC' — AND THEY BROUGHT YOU THIS FAMOUS FRANK KITCHEN.

I NEVER ADMITTED ANYTHING OF THE SORT! YOU'RE JUST TRYING TO ENTRAP ME. AND I THOUGHT WE WERE FRIENDS.

SARCASM IN YOUR SITUATION? THAT'S GREAT. SO YOU GOT FRANK AND OPERATED ON HIM AND TURNED HIM INTO A WOMAN. AGAINST HIS WILL. WHY DIDN'T YOU JUST KILL HIM?

I BELIEVE I ALREADY ANSWERED THAT QUESTION.

NOT SUFFICIENTLY ENOUGH TO PERSUADE ME THAT THIS FRANK KITCHEN REALLY EXISTS. I THINK YOU INVENTED HIM TO HIDE SOMETHING WORSE.

YOU KIDNAPPED THOSE POOR MEN BECAUSE YOU HAVE MENTAL PROBLEMS.

AH, GOD! SPARE ME THIS AMATEUR PSYCHOANALYSIS! YOU'RE NOTHING BUT SHITTY BUREAUCRA YOU TAKE YOURSEL FOR A COP? DO YO HAVE ANY IDEA WHO I AM... ?

GLEASON WASN'T TERRIBLY HARD TO FIND. HE HAD AN OFFICE, A ROUTINE, KEPT REGULAR HOURS. LIKE A LOT OF GUYS IN HIS BUSINESS, HE CULTIVATED THE AROMA OF *RESPECTABILITY*.

IN MY FIELD, THE ELEMENT OF *SURPRISE* IS OFTEN A DECISIVE ADVANTAGE. BUT IN THIS CASE, THE TARGET KNEW HE WAS IN MY SIGHTS, SO SURPRISE WAS OUT. UNLESS...

HE HAD BODYGUARDS AND SURVEILLANCE CAMERAS. BUT HAVING CAMERAS DIDN'T MEAN SOMEONE WAS WATCHING THEM EVERY MINUTE. AND WITH TIME, BODYGUARDS GET SLOPPY.

KRASH!

AT 11AM, IN BROAD DAYLIGHT, IN YOUR OFFICE, YOU FEEL SAFE. THAT'S HOW TO GET THE UPPER HAND, HOW TO REGAIN THE ELEMENT OF SURPRISE.

BLAM!

BLAM!

FRANK! IT'S REALLY YOU, ISN'T IT? YOU'RE LOOKING *ODD*, BUT I SEE YOU HAVEN'T LOST YOUR TOUCH. WHO ARE YOU WORKING FOR NOW?

MYSELF, JOHN. I WANT TO KNOW *WHAT* HAPPENE *WHY* YOU SET THAT FUCKING TRAP FOR M AND *WHO* YOU SOLD ME OUT TO.

YOU'RE AFTER THE *DOCTOR*, I SUPPOSE?

EXACTLY.

THE DOCTOR AND I, WE WERE IN BUSINESS. I SENT HER MEN, MEN NO ONE WOULD EVER MISS. SHE PAID ME 50,000 DOLLARS A HEAD. FOR YOU, IT WAS *100,000* DOLLARS. *WHY?* I HAVE NO IDEA. I DIDN'T KNOW AND I DIDN'T CARE. AT LEAST, NOT UNTIL NOW.

TELL ME MORE ABOUT THIS DOCTOR.

WE WEREN'T BUDDIES, SHE AND ME. IT WAS JUST BUSINESS. SHE CALLED ME FROM TIME TO TIME, AND SHE PAID PROMPTLY. I DON'T KNOW WHERE SHE LIVES. IN MY OPINION, SHE'S *LOONEY.* YOU WANT TO KNOW MORE ABOUT HER, ASK YOUR *GIRLFRIEND.*

IF I TOLD YOU JUST HOW *SORRY* I AM, HOW MUCH I REGRET WHAT HAPPENED, WHY I DID IT, WHERE THE DOCTOR IS... WOULD YOU STILL KILL ME?

YOU CAN ALWAYS TRY.

I DID IT FOR MONEY. I DID IT BECAUSE I HAD NO BETTER OPTIONS, AND BECAUSE I HATED THE WHOLE WORLD, MYSELF INCLUDED. I DID IT FOR ALL THE SAME SHITTY REASONS THAT NEVER TRULY JUSTIFY ANYTHING. I DID IT. THAT'S ALL.

IT WAS YOU? *YOU* WERE THE NURSE?

I COULD TELL YOU THE WHOLE STORY, BUT IT WOULDN'T CHANGE ANYTHING. I'D JUST BE MAKING EXCUSES. GO AHEAD, *KILL ME*. AT LEAST THAT WAY, IT'LL ALL BE OVER.

THE NEXT NIGHT...

I HADN'T PULLED THE TRIGGER.
I HADN'T BEEN ABLE TO. SHE'D
ASKED IF WE MIGHT STILL HAVE A
CHANCE, HER AND ME. I TOLD HER I
NEEDED TIME TO DIGEST THINGS.
I PUT HER ON A BUS TO RENO, WHERE
SHE HAD SOME FRIENDS, AND PUT PANCHO
IN A KENNEL UNTIL FURTHER NOTICE.

JOHNNIE HAD TOLD ME
EVERYTHING SHE KNEW.
THAT THE DOCTOR WAS A
REAL DOCTOR. THAT SHE'D
SAID SHE WAS HEADING UP
A PROJECT ON EXPERIMENTAL
SURGERY, NOT STRICTLY
LEGAL BUT DESTINED TO HELP
MANY PEOPLE.

SHE DIDN'T KNOW THE
DOCTOR'S REAL NAME.
APPARENTLY, THE WOMAN ALWAYS PAID
TOP DOLLAR AND ALWAYS ON THE
DOT. HER THING WAS MUTILATIONS,
OF BUMS, THE SICK, THE POOR...

AFTER THE FIRST TIME,
JOHNNIE HAD WANTED TO
QUIT, BUT IT WAS MADE
CLEAR THAT SHE MIGHT
FIND *HERSELF* ON THE
OPERATING TABLE IF
SHE TRIED IT.

SHE DIDN'T KNOW WHERE
SHE WAS BASED EITHER.
THE DOCTOR HAD BROUGHT
HER TO A DIFFERENT
LOCATION EACH TIME. BUT
SHE'D CALLED YESTERDAY...

THIS TIME, THE DOCTOR WANTED A GIRL. SHE SAID SHE'D BE PICKING UP A HOOKER ON MARKET STREET, AROUND MIDNIGHT.

I HAD A DESCRIPTION OF THE CAR: A DARK GREEN ROLLS ROYCE. SHE'D TOLD JOHNNIE TO BE READY AROUND ONE IN THE MORNING.

KEEP DRIVING, PAL. YOU CAN'T AFFORD IT.

THE ROLLS. JOHNNIE HADN'T LIED TO ME. IT WAS NOW OR NEVER.

WOW! WHAT A GREAT CAR!

I KNOW SOMEONE WHO'S LOOKING FOR COMPANY FOR THE NIGHT AND WHO'LL PAY WELL. INTERESTED?

THAT'S A HOTEL?

IT'S A LUXURY HOTEL. MY FRIEND BOUGHT AND RENOVATED IT.

SHE'S DONE SOMETHING RATHER... *UNIQUE* WITH IT. HOLD ON, THERE SHE IS.

HELLO, *FRANK*. IT'S A PLEASURE TO SEE YOU AGAIN.

JESUS...

HELLO, FRANK. I HOPE YOU SLEPT WELL. AND THAT THIS CELL AGREES WITH YOU. IT'S NOT MUCH, BUT THEN, IT'S ONLY FOR A SHORT TIME. RIGHT NOW, I THINK WE SHOULD HAVE A LITTLE CONVERSATION.

GO *FUCK* YOURSELF.

YOU DON'T EVEN KNOW WHAT I'M HERE TO TALK ABOUT, DO YOU?

I KNOW YOU BUTCHERED ME, AND ENJOYED DOING IT. I ALSO KNOW I'M GOING TO MAKE YOU PAY DEARLY FOR IT.

OF COURSE, OF COURSE. *REVENGE*, ALWAYS REVENGE. BUT IT'S *MY* REVENGE WE'RE TALKING ABOUT HERE. FOR THE DEATH OF SEBASTIAN. I LEFT YOU HIS PHOTO. DID YOU SEE IT?

SURE, I KILLED YOUR BOYFRIEND. HE OWED MONEY TO SOME BAD PEOPLE. YOU WANT ME TO TELL YOU I *REGRET* IT? I DON'T REGRET ANYTHING. IT WAS A JOB. NOTHING MORE.

SEBASTIAN WAS NOT MY *BOYFRIEND.* HE WAS MY *BROTHER.* MY LITTLE BROTHER. I LOVED HIM VERY MUCH. WE WERE VERY CLOSE. BUT I SEE I'M WASTING MY TIME TALKING WITH YOU. I'LL OPERATE ON YOU TONIGHT. I WORK BETTER AT NIGHT. UNTIL THEN, RELAX AND REFLECT ON WHAT'S ABOUT TO HAPPEN TO YOU. THAT'LL MAKE IT EVEN BETTER.

LATER THE SAME DAY...

IT'S TIME. YOU WANT ME TO UNDRESS YOU, OR CAN YOU DO IT YOURSELF?

DON'T TOUCH ME. I'LL DO IT.

NOT BAD, HUH, GUYS? THE *TITS* SHE GAVE ME?

AND I'VE GOT SOMETHING TO SHOW YOU, NURSE – I FOUND ANOTHER DOCTOR WHO SEWED ME ON A **BRAND NEW** ONE. I BET YOU'D LIKE TO SEE IT...

WHAT ARE YOU BLATHERING ABOUT? THAT'S **IMPOSSIBLE**. THE DOCTOR WON'T BE PLEASED AT ALL THAT SOMEONE ELSE HAS TOUCHED YOUR...

HEY!

THUNK

BLAM! BLAM! BLAM!

BLAM!
BLAM!

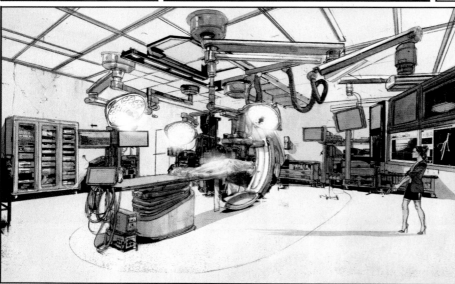

NO!

JOHNNIE...

YOU SEE, IT'S NOT BAD TO USE YOUR BRAIN. YOU SHOULD TRY IT SOMETIME. LET ME PROPOSE SOMETHING... WE'VE BOTH GOT WEAPONS – YOUR GUN, MY SCALPEL. YOU WALK AWAY AND SO DO I. WE NEVER MEET AGAIN. I GIVE YOU MY WORD.

FRANK, LISTEN TO ME. I DON' BELIEVE YOU HAVE AN' BULLETS LEFT. BUT I WON'T USE THE SCALPE FOR ANYTHING BUT SELF-DEFENSE...

WHAT ARE YOU DOING?

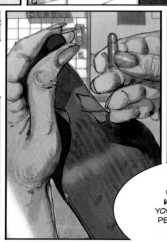

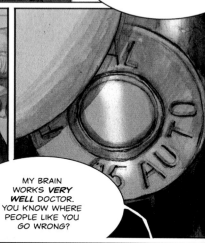

MY BRAIN WORKS VERY WELL DOCTOR. YOU KNOW WHERE PEOPLE LIKE YOU GO WRONG?

WAIT, FRANK! WAIT! D-DON'T KILL ME!

YOU THINK YOU'RE THE WORST PERSON IN THE WORLD, BU' YOU UNDERESTIMA' OTHER PEOPLE. YC THINK AFTER WHA YOU DID TO ME, AN AFTER KILLING JOHN THAT THERE'S EVEN REMOTE CHANCE I LET YOU LEAVE HERE IN ONE PIECE?

OBVIOUSLY, I DIDN'T HAVE ANYWHERE NEAR HER TECHNICAL SKILL OR MEDICAL KNOWLEDGE. I KNEW *NOTHING* ABOUT ANESTHESIA, FOR INSTANCE. SO I JUST SKIPPED IT.

IT WAS THE WORK OF AN AMATEUR, BUT I CERTAINLY PUT MY HEART INTO IT. AN EYE FOR AN EYE, A TOOTH FOR A TOOTH... MORE OR LESS.

AFTER CUTTING OFF THE DOCTOR'S FINGERS, I'D CALLED THE POLICE FROM A NEARBY BAR AND TOLD THEM TO SEND AN AMBULANCE. SHE NEVER WENT TO TRIAL. THEY JUST PUT HER AWAY IN AN INSANE ASYLUM.

I FELT BAD ABOUT JOHNNIE. SHE DESERVED BETTER. IT HAD BEEN THE FIRST AND ONLY TIME I'D ACTUALLY FELT SOMETHING FOR SOMEONE...

THE DOCTOR HAD BEEN RIGHT ABOUT ONE THING. I WASN'T A MAN ANYMORE, BUT I WASN'T ENTIRELY A WOMAN YET EITHER. FRANK KITCHEN WAS DEAD, AT ANY RATE. BUT HE HADN'T BEEN MUCH OF A GUY.

I HAVE A **PURPOSE** IN LIFE NOW. ALL THOSE MEN WHO EXPLOIT WOMEN TO MAKE EASY MONEY – I CAN DO SOMETHING ABOUT THEM. IN MY OWN WAY.

THERE ARE TONS OF WOMEN WHO LAND HERE – FROM MEXICO, FROM RUSSIA, FROM GOD-KNOWS-WHERE – BELIEVING THERE'S A JOB WAITING FOR THEM, ONLY TO FIND THEMSELVES ON THE SIDEWALK.

IT HAPPENS EVERY DAY. AND THE NEXT TIME IT DOES, I MIGHT JUST BE THERE WITH MY .45.

THIS GUY, FOR EXAMPLE. JACK CLEARY. EX-CON, LIFELONG SHIT. HE BRINGS WOMEN IN FROM THAILAND, TELLS THEM THEY'LL BE WORKING IN A NAIL SALON, THEN HE PUTS THEM ON THE STREET AND DEALS OUT BEATINGS IF THEY DON'T BRING IN ENOUGH MONEY...

... WELL, HE USED TO...

HAVE MERCY! PLEASE DON'T SHOOT ME!

GET YOUR CLOTHES. TAKE HIS MONEY. ALL OF IT. GO FAR AWAY AND NEVER COME BACK. YOU DESERVE BETTER. WE ALL DO.

COVER GALLERY

HARD CASE CRIME

"HARD CASE MAY BE THE BEST NEW AMERICAN PUBLISHER TO APPEAR IN THE LAST DECADE."
• NEAL POLLACK IN THE STRANGER

no. 1

MATZ - WALTER HILL - JEF

THE ASSIGNMENT

川名菜

金录景

MOTEL

COVER A - JEF

ISSUE 1

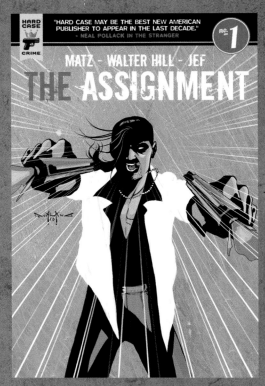

COVER B - PASQUALE QUALANO

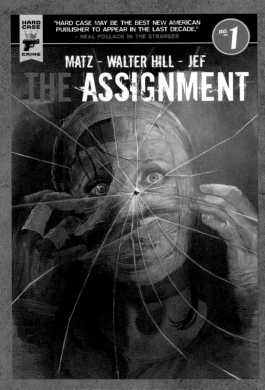

COVER C - FAY DALTON

COVER D - STEVE SCOTT

COVER E - FRANCISCO PARONZINI

ISSUE 2

COVER A - ALEX SHIBAO

COVER B - SIMONE DI MEO

COVER C - JEF

COVER D - JEF

ISSUE 3

COVER A - ALEX SHIBAO

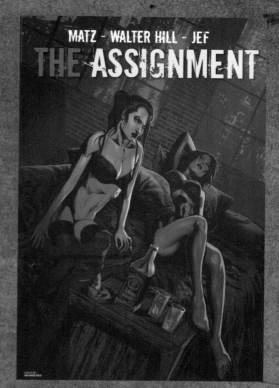

COVER B - WAGNAR REIS

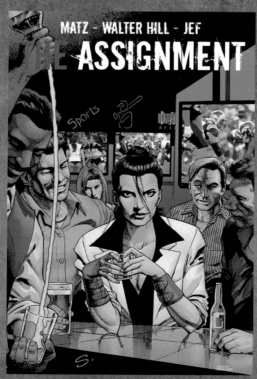

COVER C - STEVE SCOTT

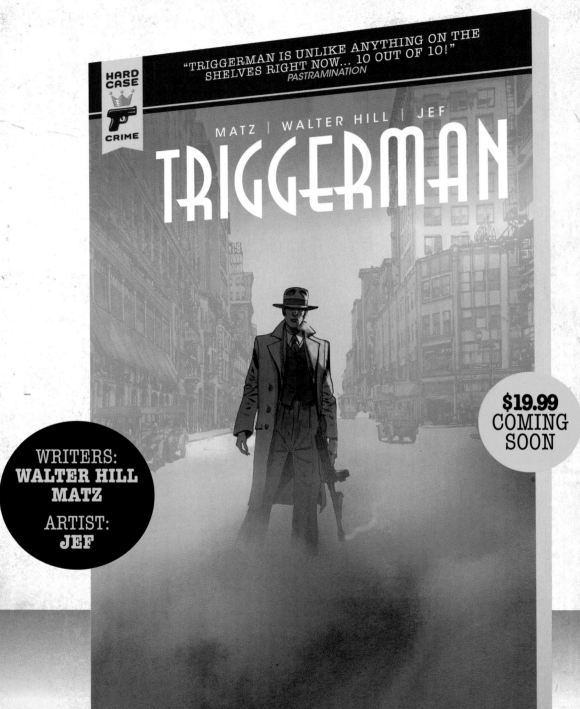

For information on how to subscribe to our Hard Case Crime titles, or to purchase them digitally, visit:
WWW.TITAN-COMICS.COM

TITAN

Originally published as *Balles perdues*. © 2015 Rue de Sèvres, Paris / The name 'Hard Case Crime' and the Hard Case Crime logo are trademarks of Winterfall LLC.

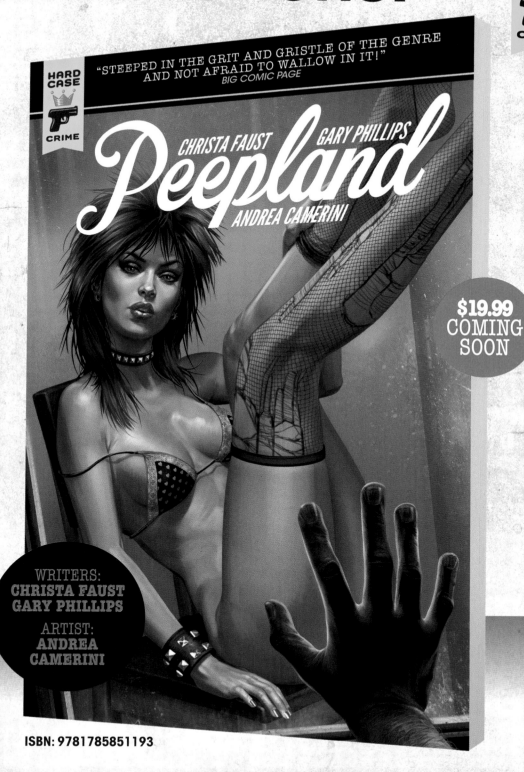

BIOS

WALTER HILL

is an American film director, screenwriter, and producer. He is widely known for his action films including, *The Warriors, Hard Times, The Driver, Southern Comfort, 48 Hrs.* and its sequel *Another 48 Hrs., Red Heat, Last Man Standing, Undisputed,* and *Bullet to the Head,* as well as writing the Steve McQueen crime drama *The Getaway*. Recently branching out into the comics world, Hill's debut title is the prohibition era crime epic, *Triggerman*.

MATZ

(also known as Alexis Nolent) is a French writer. He writes scripts for videogames and has also written a novel and, under the Matz pen-name, a number of comics, including *Triggerman* by Walter Hill. His graphic novel, *Du plomb dans la tête*, AKA *Headshot* was adapted into the 2012 film, *Bullet to the Head*.

JEF

(also known as Jean-François Martinez and Nino) is a French comics artist and designer who has illustrated several titles including *Hunt, Jim Morrison: Poet of Chaos, Garous* and *Triggerman*.